THE PHILIPPINES

A JOURNEY THROUGH THE ARCHIPELAGO

PHILIP

THE PINES

A JOURNEY THROUGH THE ARCHIPELAGO

SEVEN DAYS IN THE PHILIPPINES
WITH **35** OF THE WORLD'S
FINEST PHOTOGRAPHERS

OCTOBER 8TH–14TH, 1995

JONATHAN BEST
Early Images

JAMES HAMILTON-PATERSON
History Tells The Story

RODRIGO D. PEREZ III
Chapter Introductions

ALEJANDRO R. ROCES
Fiesta Islands

ELIZABETH V. REYES
Captions

Archipelago Press

Endpapers: A bird in flight across the waters of Palawan.
RIO HELMI

First page: A smiling Filipina waves the flag.

Previous pages: An aerial view of a seaweed farm in the Sulu Archipelago reveals an important cottage industry of the Badjao.
RIO HELMI

Opposite: On a clear day you can see rice paddies forever. Rice paddies grown by the wetland method feed almost 70 million mouths a day in the Philippines.
GUIDO ALBERTO ROSSI

Contents page: Leyte's heroic moment in bronze. The MacArthur Monument depicts the World War II American landing at Leyte.

Following pages: The perfect shape of Mount Mayon rises to the sky. This volcano has erupted nearly 50 times since 1616.
ROBIN MOYER

The T'boli tribespeople living around Lake Sebu in Mindanao cross the water in small bancas and pause to gather edible flowers.
BRUNO BARBEY

Sunset in Luzon: another day comes to a close in the northern Philippines.
MICHAEL S. YAMASHITA

PHOTO CREDITS
for Early Images
The stereoscope on page 20 is the property of Editions Didier Millet.
The image on page 18 is reproduced by kind permission of the National Museum, Manila.
All remaining photographs are reproduced by kind permission of the Silva Collection (where indicated) or otherwise of the Author.

PUBLISHING TEAM
PUBLISHER
Didier Millet

PROJECT DIRECTOR
Marina Mahathir

COUNTRY PROJECT MANAGER
Henrietta Bolinao

EDITORIAL DIRECTOR
Peter Schoppert

PROJECT EDITOR
Jill A. Laidlaw

DESIGN
Steve Page

MAP ARTWORK
Anuar Abdulrahim

PHOTO EDITORS
Marie-Claude Millet
Janie Joseland Bennett
Assistant: Nico T. Lewis

EDITORIAL CONSULTANT
Alfredo Roces

BUSINESS MANAGER
Charles Orwin

PRODUCTION
Edmund Lam

PROJECT ACCOUNTANT
Shirley Low

PHOTOGRAPHIC ASSIGNMENTS
Host Photographer: Richard Baldovino
Chief Assignment Coordinator: Raul Teehankee
Assignment Coordinators: Angie De Silva, JoJo De Veyra, Susan Del Mundo, Joel Sol Cruz, Alex Hontiveros, Amiel Martin, Bobot Meru, Maningning Miclat, Tommy Ng, Justin Nuyda, Elizabeth V. Reyes, Paul Sison, Larry Sison

TRAVEL AND LOGISTICS
Irene Tan

© 1996 Archipelago Press, an imprint of Editions Didier Millet
64 Peck Seah Street
Singapore 079325

Reprinted in 1997, 1999

Color separation by Colourscan, Singapore, printed by Tien Wah Press, Singapore

ISBN: 981-3018-99-2

14

EARLY IMAGES

Jonathan Best

34

HISTORY TELLS

THE STORY

James Hamilton-Paterson

CONTENTS

46

CHAPTER ONE

BEAUTY & BOUNTY

86

CHAPTER TWO

SOUL & HISTORY

134

CHAPTER THREE

LIFE'S WORK

190

CHAPTER FOUR

THE ART OF JOY

APPENDICES

Fiesta Islands **234**

21 Filipino Things **239**

Map of the Journey **242**

Diary of the Journey **243**

The Photographers **246**

The Authors **250**

Photography Index **251**

The Sponsors **252**

Logistics and Support **254**

Acknowledgements **255**

ROMEO GACAD

- A. SORIANO CORPORATION
- AYALA CORPORATION
- COCA-COLA BOTTLERS PHILIPPINES, INC.
- DEVELOPMENT BANK OF THE PHILIPPINES
- DUTY FREE PHILIPPINES
- EQUITABLE BANKING CORPORATION
- *INTERNATIONAL HERALD TRIBUNE*
- JAKA GROUP
- MERALCO
- NATIONAL STEEL CORPORATION
- PEARL FARM BEACH RESORT
- PETRON CORPORATION
- PHILIPPINE AMUSEMENT AND GAMING CORPORATION
- PHILIPPINE CHARITY SWEEPSTAKES OFFICE
- *PHILIPPINE DAILY INQUIRER*
- PHILIPPINE LONG DISTANCE COMPANY
- PILIPINAS SHELL CORPORATION
- PUERTO AZUL LAND, INC.
- RUSTAN'S
- SAN MIGUEL CORPORATION
- YUCHENGCO GROUP OF COMPANIES

EARLY
CAPTURING
IMAGES
LIGHT

A 'Sangley' Filipina, one of the many beautiful portraits Alfred Marche took to Paris from Manila in the early 1880's.

Photography was first popularized in Europe with the invention of the daguerreotype in 1839. Images were captured on small metal plates and sealed under glass in decorative cases. This was a complicated process which required people to sit motionless for long periods of time in fixed poses and for photographers to work with fragile equipment and often dangerous chemicals to produce a single unique picture. Although millions of these small portraits and occasional views were taken in the cities of Europe and America during the early years of photography, the technology was not well suited for travel and images from countries far from Europe and North America are extremely rare.

A young flower vendor posing for the camera around 1900.

The Daguerreotype

Daguerreotypes dominated the first decade-and-a-half of photography during the 1840's and early 1850's; few examples from the Philippines are believed to have survived although it is known that daguerreotype photographers were working here as early as the 1840's. A daguerreotype portrait of an American photographer who worked in Manila, Mr. W. W. Wood, came up for auction a few years ago in New York, and another intriguing example, showing the walls of the old city of Manila in the early 1840's, is reported to be in a private collection in Paris. Hopefully more of these will be discovered hidden away in safe places. The problem with daguerreotypes has always been that they are especially vulnerable to the effects of tropical heat and humidity, which causes them to tarnish beyond recognition.

The Wet-Plate Collodion

Photographic technology advanced rapidly and by 1850 the wet-plate collodion process made it possible to capture a negative image on a glass plate. This could then be used to develop multiple positive copies on paper from the original negative. The process was still cumbersome, requiring cart-loads of equipment, heavy glass plates and a need to develop negatives immediately after exposure. The photographer had to fix the images chemically while they were still wet with emulsion wherever he happened to be taking his pictures.

Previous pages: View of the Binondo Canal crowded with bancas in the late 1870's.

Despite this, photographers set out from Europe and America to capture all the fabled sites of the world, from the pyramids of Egypt to the temples of Japan. From the negatives they brought back they were able to publish elegant albums and limited edition travel books illustrated with actual photographs. Men such as Francis Firth went to Egypt and Jerusalem to photograph ancient religious sites, Samuel Bourne traveled through India and the Himalayas with literally dozens of coolies carrying his photographic equipment, and John Thomson visited Cambodia in 1861 and Singapore in 1864, before eventually settling in Hong Kong until 1869. John Thomson's studies of life in China are not only magnificent examples of early Asian landscapes and city views but also poignant commentaries on the brutal living conditions in China at that time. In the 1850's and 1860's the Philippines did not attract the great names of early travel photography, but photo studios were beginning to open on the Escolta, nineteenth century Manila's most fashionable shopping street, and by the end of the 1860's several very talented photographers were at work.

The Carte-de-Visite

The most popular photographic format had now become the 'carte-de-visite.' This was a small inexpensive two-and-a-quarter by three-and-a-half inch paper print mounted on cardboard, very often with the photographer's fancy logo and studio address on the back (below). These were usually portraits which could be given as personal mementos or left at homes in place of 'visiting cards' from which they took their name. Rich Filipinos and the Spanish and *mestizo* (half Chinese, half Filipino) upper classes living in Manila were eager to have their pictures taken and to give copies to friends and relatives. This was also the first photographic format to fit easily into family albums, which made them very popular.

Cartes-de-visite were also produced as souvenirs for tourists and visitors to Manila. The photographer W. W. Wood (and later his sons) made a fine series of images called *Typos de Manila*.

These were artfully posed studio portraits of Filipinos at various trades, such as milk vendors and fruit vendors; or pictures of 'warriors' from the minority tribes, such as Negrito bowmen and the Muslim and tribal peoples of Mindanao. Other studios such as that of Pedro Picon and Albert Honiss did similar work catering to both the local elite

Crowds gathering in Manila for the inauguration of the first president, Manuel Roxas, on May 28th, 1946.

who could afford to have their portraits taken and to those foreigners curious to see pictures of the many different 'exotic types' of inhabitants in the Philippine Archipelago.

Capturing Disaster

On the evening of June 3rd, 1863, a great earthquake struck Manila, destroying many of its Spanish-style stone and tile public buildings, and the fine homes of the rich colonialists—a 'divine judgement' that did not go unnoticed by the traditional Filipinos who still lived in secure houses of flexible bamboo and nipa palm. The results of this earthquake were documented by local photographers whose prints were transformed into engravings for newspaper and magazine illustrations around the world. Pictures of collapsed buildings were taken with the newly invented twin-lens stereo camera. Similar to a person's two eyes, this camera made two almost identical images which, when seen together through a special viewer, appeared three-dimensional.

In the years following the earthquake, British resident photographer Albert Honiss, who had an establishment on the Escolta, took exceptionally beautiful pictures in and around Manila and of the flourishing trading ports of Iloilo and Cebu in the central Philippines. The American hemp exporters Russell and Sturgis assigned him in the late 1860's or early 1870's to photograph their numerous company buildings, warehouses and residences throughout the islands. Albert Honiss produced artistically composed and sharply focused albumen prints which were the equal of any work being done in Europe or America at the time. Along with his standard three-by-five inch and eight-by-ten inch images Honiss also created expertly executed multi-frame panorama views. He captured the Pasig River crowded with tall-masted ships, the formidable walls of Intramuros, the fortified

Spanish section of Manila, and the quaint farms and rice fields of the small towns of Ermita and Malate—sights which have long since vanished with the passage of time and Manila's tremendous and rapid expansion.

The opening of the Suez Canal and Spain's easing of foreign trade restrictions with the Philippines in the late 1860's brought new prosperity and an influx of foreign merchants and visitors. The carte-de-visite was replaced in the 1870's by the larger and more elegant cabinet card portrait and large format outdoor views became popular. Aside from the few commercial studios which placed identifying names and logos on the backs of their pictures, photographers rarely signed their work or were credited in publications. There were numerous itinerant foreign photographers with studios in Manila, Cebu and Iloilo, men from America, England, France and Italy, and *Peninsulares* (Spanish-born colonizers), but their individual work is hard to identify and occasionally they lent or sold each other negatives and prints.

Filipino Photographic Skill

It is unclear how much of the photographic work may actually have been done by Filipino Indios, as the Spanish then called the majority of the people of the Philippines, or by native Chinese Filipinos. The developing and printing of cabinet cards and larger photo albums required many skilled craftsmen and it can be assumed that the bulk of this work was being done by local Filipinos. The Spanish colonials born in the Philippines and known as *Insulares* were not accustomed to doing any work which required manual labor.

Filipina Portraits

A Frenchman named Alfred Marche lived in Manila between 1879 and 1885 and took back to Paris an exquisite collection of photographic portraits of Filipino women. He carefully documented the various types of ethnic Filipinas, from aristocratic Spanish-mestizas to charming young women from rich Malay Filipino families and stunningly beautiful Chinese-Spanish or Chinese-Malay 'Sangley' Filipinas. For centuries Chinese traders

A pair of American soldiers posing at a fashionable Manila photo studio, circa 1902. Many US servicemen posed for photographs to send home from America's first and last colony.

Above: A Francisco Van Camp photograph of the bell tower of Manila cathedral after the earthquake of 1880.

Right: A stereoscope of a man with antiquated Spanish cannons on the walls of Intramuros, Manila. During the late nineteenth century and well into this century stereoscopic slides were popular novelty items. If a photograph was taken with a camera with two lenses mounted at approximately the same distance apart as human eyes, the resulting images, when viewed with a special viewer or 'stereoscope', appear three-dimensional.

had been coming to the Manila Bay port of Sangley near Cavite where they settled and raised families, producing their 'Sangley' offspring.

These women are pictured wearing the traditional *saya* or skirt in bold patterns over which a more subtle *tapiz* is wrapped. They wear almost transparent, beautifully decorated blouses of abaca or *piña*, a pineapple fiber, and are modestly covered with finely embroidered *panuelos* wrapped loosely around their shoulders. Their costumes are completed with painted Chinese fans, decorative tortoise-shell and gold hair combs, religious scapulas and delicate gold filigree necklaces and rings. During this period Filipino women treated their luxuriant and abundant hair with scented coconut oil and often proudly wore it down—quite an impressive sight as it sometimes reached their slippers.

A formal portrait of General Emilio Aguinaldo, 1898.

Press Photographs

One of Alfred Marche's friends in Manila was an Italian photographer named Antonio Perello who had a studio at 22 Escolta and may have been the photographer of the Filipina beauties. Perello's second-floor studio was wrecked by a second great earthquake which struck in July of 1880. The collapsed interior of the studio is recorded in the earthquake pictures of photographer Francisco Van Camp, a neighbor of Perello's at 35 Escolta. Van Camp ran Manila's most successful studio at the time, turning out cabinet cards for his regular clientele and albums for select collectors. His series of photos on the effects of the 1880 earthquake were reproduced as engravings in *Harper's Weekly Magazine* in New York and the *Illustrated London News* in England that same year.

Van Camp also made studies of local street scenes and characteristic groups of people. He posed vendors outdoors displaying their wares, people next to their shops, people drying fish, selling carabao milk or just sitting in family groups, usually several generations together with shy servants peeking from around corners or hidden behind foliage. The long exposure time still made the poses appear stiff and somewhat unnatural, but these were a definite improvement over the small format studio studies of the previous generation.

In the Philippines, as elsewhere, one of the ironies of photography in a colonial context was that photographers often used stock studio backdrops which were popular in Europe at the time. This pleased the rich clientele who sought out the latest in European fashion, but was disconcerting when used in studies of people wearing traditional Filipino costumes or tribal attire, or lacking it. Negrito bow-men or Bagobo *datus* (lords) posed against romantic Alpine backdrops with Victorian props such as classical Greek columns, rustic park benches, or love seats must have seemed comical at the time. They are fitting evidence of the cultural confrontations that were taking place during the nineteenth century.

The 1880's saw the first use of photographs in an anthropological expedition to the Philippines. Before 1880 a few European travelers such as Marche had come to the Philippines and assembled small collections of photos as examples of the people living there. In 1887, and again in 1890, Dean C. Worcester from the University of Michigan in the United States and his companions Drs. Joseph B. Steere and Frank Bourns came and started a photographic survey of ethnic types from Mindanao to Bontoc. Worcester with his Filipino assistant collected thousands of images which he used for his own studies and as illustrations for his books, numerous articles about the Philippines which appeared in *National Geographic Magazine* and other publications, and for display at the 1904 Saint Louis World's Fair.

American Images

Dean C. Worcester turned out to be a precursor of an American invasion which overwhelmed the Philippines eleven years after his first expedition. Worcester himself played a major role in the American colonization both as a Philippine Commission member and later as an appointed government official. His early photos of the tribal peoples of Mindanao, Jolo and the Cordillera region were used for many years as misleading examples of how primitive and backward the Philippines were. Contrary to the truism that 'a picture never lies', photographs by Worcester and other often well-intentioned anthropological photographers

A rare albumen print of workers in a tobacco press in the 1880's.

*A*pplying labels to cigars, Manila factory workers, 1905.

were manipulated and miscaptioned for political reasons to justify the American military presence.

Over three centuries of Spanish colonial administration ended in the Philippines in the late 1890's. The Philippine revolution of 1896, inspired by the anti-clerical patriot Dr. Jose Rizal and led by General Emilio Aguinaldo, weakened the Spanish who were eventually driven out by the American Navy in 1898. This in turn led to an American war with the Filipinos and the eventual setting up of America's first and last colony in Asia. These traumatic and historic events were all well documented and reported photographically in one of the first fully photographed wars.

Spanish Images

In addition to beautiful nature studies, the Spanish Filipino photographer Manuel Arias Rodriguez took numerous pictures of the military conflict between the Spanish and the Filipinos prior to and during the American invasion. His collection of several hundred superb prints from this period from 1892 to 1899 were recently discovered in Madrid and have been returned to Manila in time for the 1996 centennial of the Philippine revolution.

The arrival of the American military in 1898 and the subsequent establishment of an American colonial administration in 1901 brought with it a whole new era in Philippine photography. Photographers accompanied newspaper and magazine reporters intent on covering the military and political events and also providing the American people with a visual portrait of their 'new possessions.' American soldiers, teachers and tourists arrived with new and inexpensive Kodak box cameras, taking pictures for their scrapbooks or having their film printed directly as postcards, hundreds of thousands of which were produced. Photography quickly moved from the realm of the fancy studio photographer and artistic 'amateur' to that of the documentary photographer and the truly popular art form of snapshots and postcards.

A Photography Boom

American photographers such as James Ricalton, working for the Underwood & Underwood news services and Charles Martin, assigned to be the first official government photographer in the

An oval portrait of a servant in an embroidered barong, or shirt, early 1880's.

early years of this century, took thousands of images which were used in newspapers, books and magazines throughout the United States, the Philippines and the rest of the world. The new prosperity brought by the Americans and the economic boom in Asia during the First World War in Europe gave rise to a tremendous demand for photos. Studios opened up from the newly built mountain resort of Baguio in the north to Zamboanga in Mindanao; a surprising number of these were run by Japanese, catering to foreign tourists but even more so to middle-class Filipinos who wanted their portraits taken as keepsakes.

The Camera Never Lies?

Nineteenth and early twentieth century photography in the Philippines was dominated by foreigners. The technology was imported as were most of the practitioners. It can be argued that these men brought with them prejudices both cultural and racial which in some ways distorted or limited their view of the life of the majority of Filipinos. This is certainly true, but what these photographers may have lacked individually in sensitivity to local culture they made up for collectively as documentary artists.

Viewed as a collective body of work starting in the 1850's and proceeding through the 1930's, photographers working in the Philippines have bequeathed a rich visual history of a fascinating and diverse nation. Working under difficult physical conditions and limited access to necessary supplies, chemicals and equipment, and subjected to a myriad collection of local Filipino class, racial and religious prejudices, they managed to present an exceptionally broad range of subject matter and ethnic material.

Photography is an art form and not an exact science despite its uncanny ability to reproduce what appears to be fact. An image taken for one generation of viewers might reveal a truth which takes on a different meaning for the next generation. Although the photographers who captured the nineteenth century images we enjoy today have passed from the scene, as have the people and even many of the places in their pictures, these images are still alive for us, informing and enriching our lives. They are a reflection of a time long gone but, due to photography, still immediately accessible to us. **J.B.**

A view down the Escolta towards Santa Cruz Church in the late 1870's by Francisco Van Camp. Silva Collection

The lighthouse at the mouth of the Pasig River. Visitors to Manila were sometimes greeted by musicians as they arrived by boat. Silva Collection

Above: A noon-time view of downtown Cebu in 1919, long before it became the booming metropolis it is today.

View of the crowded modern Escolta in the 1920's, looking toward Santa Cruz Church.

Right: A group of
Bagobos from southern
Mindanao around
1904, posing in their
traditional beaded and
hand-woven costumes.

Far right: An elegant
Muslim wedding in
Jolo, 1930's. The cos-
tumes and gifts make
up an eclectic mix of
Chinese, Middle
Eastern and Western
styles from the fancy
Chinese headdress of
the bride to her patent
leather high-
heeled pumps.

Right: Woman weaver
in northern Ilocos,
1905. Photographed
by Charles Martin for
the newly formed
Government Bureau
of Science.

Far right: Market
women in Cebu, 1919.

A souvenir postcard
portrait sent by Nena
in Tayabas to her
friend Rufina in
Nueva Ecija, 1930's.

A family portrait by
Francisco Van Camp,
1880's. Note the
servant peeking
through the foliage
at the center of the
image.
Silva Collection

Right: A studio study of a fruit vendor by W. W. Wood, Manila, 1860's.

Far right: Harp and guitar players, La Union Province. Carte-de-visite by Pedro Picon, 1860's.

A trick photo from the 1930's showing the same man in five different exposures.

Studio portrait of a young Chinese-Filipino with his saxophone, late 1920's.

These schoolgirls under the spreading banyan tree are students of St. William's Institute in Magsingal, a coastal town of Ilocos Sur.

HISTORY TELLS THE STORY

1

Over the last 20 years the Philippines has often had a bad press. Much of this—though not all—has been undeserved, and is due to ignorance and misconception. In fact, a case could be made for calling this the least understood country in Southeast Asia precisely *because* it seems so accessible to Western visitors (being largely Christian and largely English speaking). The camera, too, can make it look as richly exotic as anywhere else in the region. Yet to view the Philippines as a series of empty visual images will be once again to misunderstand what is seen. To look at it without being aware of its extraordinary history will be to see a society which makes very little sense, as well as one which cannot fairly reflect its future prospects. Any visitor will soon observe that in some fundamental way this country is quite unlike its neighbors. For that matter, the Philippines is like nowhere else on earth, which ought to be the discerning traveler's highest accolade.

2

Philippine history starts badly in that there are no indigenous accounts of the archipelago and its people prior to its conquest by Spain. Until recently, the country's history was that of its colonizers, written by foreigners in a foreign tongue. In 1521 Ferdinand Magellan, the Portuguese adventurer then working for Spain, notified the Spanish Crown of these islands' existence. Twenty years went by before they were officially named 'Las Islas Filipinas' in honor of Philip II, heir apparent to the Hapsburg throne. In 1565, the first permanent Spanish settlement was established in Cebu (now the major city of the Visayan region) before the colonial capital was finally moved to Manila in 1571.

The settlers soon discovered they faced an administrative nightmare: an archipelago of over 7,000 islands inhabited by people largely of Malay stock but subdivided into hundreds of tribes, ethnic groupings and distinct languages. There were already centuries-old links with Indian, Japanese and Chinese traders, while the treacherous seas dotted with jungled islets were home to the junks and craft of pirate raiders.

From the first, the Spaniards' colonization of this archipelago was quite different from their conquest of Latin America. The sheer distance of Manila from Madrid meant a journey via Mexico; and for the next two centuries and more, the galleon supply route sailed unreliably between the Philippines and Acapulco. The new country thus became, in a manner of speaking, the colony of a colony (it was actually administered as a Mexican province). These thinly stretched lines of communication restricted the numbers of travelers, so there was no mass migration of adventurers, bureaucrats and military from Spain. This in turn meant that the Philippines was never really conquered in its entirety. None but the most zealous missionary could penetrate to the mountain tribes living in remote isolation in the high Cordillera, while the thinly spread military soon gave up hoping to subdue the 'moors' in the Muslim south, in Sulu and parts of Mindanao.

There, the local datus and petty sultanates were far too well entrenched, trading from easily-defended fiefdoms up sheltered estuaries amid thick jungle. And there they still were, not much changed, when Joseph Conrad described them in his novels at the turn of the twentieth century. Even today, people in certain parts of the country still refer to the *habagat*—the southwest monsoon—as the "pirate wind", commemorating the local communities' fear of the seasonal gales which brought crews of marauding Moros up from their southern strongholds, attacking the galleon trade and carrying off slaves even from the northernmost parts of Luzon. Many of the watchtowers the locals built in defence can still be seen.

A second factor lay behind the peculiar way in which the country came under Spanish rule. Unlike in South America, there were no myths of El Dorado, no great mines of silver and precious stones. There is mineral wealth in the Philippines, to be sure, but not of the kind that inspires gold rushes. As a result, there were no greedy conquistadores looting the country from end to end. Instead—and uniquely—it was largely subdued and administered by *los frailes,* friars of various Catholic orders whose official task was that of conversion. The Spanish Crown's grandly ambitious aim was the spiritual conquest of Japan and China, and only incidentally that of the Philippines, which was viewed more as a stepping stone. Describing himself as "an instrument of Divine Providence," Philip II regarded it as a matter of moral scruple that this "barbaric archipelago" should be won for Christ by the Bible rather than by the sword. A measure of this mission's success is that the Philippines became, and remains today, Southeast Asia's only predominantly Christian country. This on its own would make it singular and ensure it a later history very different from that of other colonized countries in the region.

From the late sixteenth until the late nineteenth centuries, therefore, the Philippines was effectively run by a foreign church. The task these Spanish friars, thousands of

miles from home, had set themselves was prodigious: nothing less than the 'cultural cleansing' of an entire population. The early priests soon found that a widely understood written syllabary already existed, belying their charges of barbarianism, but they marginalized this writing system as inadequate and replaced it with the Castilian alphabet. The islanders' old tribal pantheons of gods, the deep-rooted animistic beliefs, were likewise to be eliminated. Unfamiliar Christian rituals were conducted in yet another new tongue—Latin.

This process took a long, long time. As is now apparent, it was never wholly achieved. After initial strides in promoting such things as literacy and the ideals of European humanism, the years passed and the modernizing impetus became stagnant. The Philippines increasingly became a cultural backwater. Things began to change once more only in the nineteenth century, when the country grudgingly opened itself to international trade.

Yet even as economic pressures brought about the first decisive political shifts, social practices remained far behind the times. As late as the 1890's an American visitor to Manila was astonished to be able to witness public garrottings: festive occasions eagerly watched by crowds which included dainty young ladies giggling in their Sunday best. He noted drily that much worse could be seen any day in the provinces.

Inevitably, a system so entrenched and so far from Spain's supervision had long since become corrupt. By the mid-nineteenth century the friarocracy had fallen very far from its founders' ideals. The various Orders now owned huge tracts of land and wielded absolute power over the Indios as well as over the Spanish military and civil governors. The Church bled the already impoverished peasants still further with tithes and taxes and indulgences. Many of the friars kept mistresses and had illegitimate children. Indeed, a large proportion of the mestizo blood in modern Filipinos' veins comes from those avowedly celibate men of God. No matter that there had always been among the priests men

A tiny Manobo girl in festive costume attends a Thanksgiving Festival in the village of Mawig, 15 kilometers outside Cotabato City.

of great saintliness, humanity and courage. Well before the end of the century there were popular revolts and uprisings against the brutality and hypocrisy of individual friars and their local regimes.

3

Today's visitor to the Philippines will find, in practically every town of the archipelago, a statue of the national hero, Jose Rizal. Viewed historically, Rizal was one of the great Asian nationalists of the same generation—he, Gandhi, Tagore and Sun Yat Sen all being born in the 1860's. Yet Rizal was unique, and would have been so in any country at any time. His middle class provincial boyhood nurtured a great poetic sensibility, while his intellectual achievement when still a teenager turned out to be crucial to his country's subsequent history.

By the end of the nineteenth century, and in spite of the friars' conservatism, increased trading links with Europe had produced a growing mestizo middle class. For some years a number of ilustrados (educated Filipinos) had been traveling abroad to finish their studies, and had seen for themselves how underdeveloped their own country remained. Yet, despite their observations and the rumblings of discontent among the common people, probably no one until Rizal had made the intellectual leap of blaming the friarocracy itself for this state of affairs. It might be hard to believe today, but it is a measure of the absolute power the Catholic Church wielded over the minds of its flock. It was not only a difficult thought to have had at the time, but a dangerous one. To blame the friars *en masse* was to blame the Mother Church herself and, by implication, Spain, thereby adding sedition to the crime of blasphemy. While still a very young man, Rizal had a painful insight (which he tried to keep from his conventionally-minded parents for fear of offending them) that what was wrong with his beloved country was not the abuses of individual friars but the entire system whereby the Philippines was ruled by foreigners.

Rizal was himself partly excited and partly scared by his own conclusion. Restlessly, and convinced his life would be short, he resolved to learn as much as he could about his country and its distant "motherland." While training as a doctor he twice traveled to Europe, a typical ilustrado, talking to groups of his fellow exiles but also meeting and befriending scholars all over the continent and becoming fluent in several languages. He left all who met him deeply impressed and moved by his brillance and determination.

He returned home more than ever certain his country would not develop further until it was free of Spain and the friars. He wanted nothing less than independence. His conviction had been reinforced by seeing Spain, Germany, France and England for himself. He was appalled at how far Manila lagged behind Madrid in terms of intellectual freedom, while he likened the Philippine provinces to a medieval dungeon. He wrote two powerful novels— *Noli Me Tangere* and *El Filibusterismo*— whose revolutionary message added notoriety to the literary fame they earned him. Yet Rizal himself always drew back from calling publicly for revolution, and still more from advocating armed struggle. Maybe he went on believing in a Spanish benevolence and good sense that would make a gradual transition possible without bloody confrontation.

To the end, the friarocracy was stubborn. The civilized man of letters, the man who had never so much as lifted a sword in anger (though he was an accomplished fencer) was condemned to death for treason. On December 30th, 1896, having spent the last night in his cell writing his most famous poem, Jose Rizal was publicly shot in the back by a firing squad—a traitor's death—on the seafront overlooking Manila Bay. The exact spot is marked today by his monument in the Luneta Park. He was 35. From their point of view, this callous act turned out to be the worst thing the Spanish could have done, though from Rizal's it was his crowning achievement. On the instant he became a martyr, his suffering and sacrifice popularly likened to that of Christ. His ideas flew like wildfire. Local uprisings turned into mass revolt, and it was not long before a

The Rizal Monument in Luneta Park appropriately marks the heart of Manila.

revolutionary Filipino government was established and sworn in at Malolos, Bulacan, a town which briefly became the capital of the short-lived first Philippine Republic.

If poetic justice really existed, the poet Rizal's story ought rightly to end with the overthrow of the colonial administration and the creation of an independent Philippines. But fairytale endings are everywhere in short supply. At the time, the United States was embroiled in the Spanish-American war, which had not been concerned with the Philippines at all, but with Cuba. Now, seeing the chance of advantage, the Americans offered the Filipino nationalist forces a deal. In exchange for their help in routing the Spanish from the archipelago, they said, the United States would ensure the Philippines' independence. Barely two years after Rizal's execution, Commodore Dewey sank the Spanish fleet in Manila Bay and Spain's three-and-a-half centuries' hegemony was over. Yet the Filipinos who had fought decisively to help the Americans rid them of their mutual enemy were suddenly astonished to discover that the United States was reneging on the deal. Their new allies had no intention of leaving. Expansionists in Washington were viewing the Philippines as a stepping stone (how history repeats itself!) for American exporters with an eye on the "Great China Market" (then as now). Once they had set up their administration, the Americans turned their attention to mopping up their former comrades in arms whom they now labeled "rebels".

At this point the class divisions in Filipino society showed through. In the power vacuum that formed in the wake of the defeated Spanish, the mestizo hacienda owners and middle class ilustrados made it clear they vastly preferred that Americans should fill it rather than what they saw as an illiterate, rag-tag Filipino peasantry. For the collective psyche the whole episode was a stunning betrayal, and one which many Filipinos still feel set the tone of their country's fortunes over these last 100 years. A ruthless war ensued.

By the end, over 4,000 American and 16,000 Filipino troops had lost their lives, while 200,000 civilians were dead, mainly of disease and starvation.

Like the Spanish before them, the Americans found they had inherited a daunting territory. Their troops and administrators found themselves balked by densely jungled mountains slashed by deep ravines, as well as by thousands of scattered islands where communication was dependent

GUEORGUI PINKHASSOV

on boats, which in turn were subject to availability and weather. It is easy for a modern visitor to appreciate the problem. Today, the jungles may have receded but the mountains and ravines, the sea and the weather remain unchanged. Even nowadays, the capital feels remote to most people living in the provinces. People live out their lives without directly experiencing much of the power Manila wields, let alone seeing the city for themselves.

Yet terrain was not the only reason why the Americanization of the Philippines took longer than expected. Back in Washington many concerned voices were raised against a new adventurism which was widely seen as undemocratic. They said it was mere hypocrisy to preach freedom for "little brown brothers" while helping American companies take over valuable friar lands. In fact, the Democratic Party's platform was for the Philippines' immediate independence—a proposal the Republican President Theodore Roosevelt successfully resisted. Here was a sign of a deep ambivalence about their respective roles, which in one way or another has dogged both countries ever since. Were the Americans liberators or the new enslavers? Were the Filipinos beneficiaries or finally losers in the deal? Certainly, many Filipinos then and later were not nationalists at all, and yearned only for the day when the United States would confer statehood on their archipelago, absorbing it completely. (If Hawaii, they were to argue later, why not the Philippines?) Others, men of principle as well as the disaffected, brooded uneasily on President McKinley's notion of "benevolent assimilation" as well as on the implications of "Manifest Destiny."

Quiapo Church bursts with streamers of flags—a fitting decoration for one of Manila's most popular places of worship.

4

Historians have blamed General Douglas MacArthur for not taking full advantage, in late 1941, of the ten hours' warning he had after the Japanese attacked Pearl Harbor. Certainly the Japanese caught his small air force unprepared and on the ground. They landed along the western coasts of Zambales and Pangasinan, and the Bataan peninsula soon fell. The surviving American troops, most of whom were Filipinos, were walked in the notorious 237-kilometer Death March to concentration camps in Tarlac. Thousands died in terrible circumstances in the first months of the war. General MacArthur fled from his stronghold on Corregidor Island in Manila Bay, vowing to return. By early 1942 the Philippines once more found itself subject to a new foreign government, a new colonial power.

The fact that Filipinos were now caught up in World War II only gave a painful urgency to old issues. Now whose side were they on? Did the Filipino best serve his or her country by collaborating with these new Japanese masters, or by resisting them? Was the patriotic Filipino a quasi-American or—at some deeper level—a patriot of a nation that so far existed only in dreams? It was a profound moral dilemma. Younger visitors to these islands today might think these are long-dead, academic issues, but that would be naive. (They have only to look at France, where the issue of who collaborated with the Nazi invaders is still very much alive.) National traumas have a habit of living on, even when most of the population has no direct memory of them.

In World War II, many Filipinos did take to the hills to resist the Japanese, some of them joining their compatriots who before the war had violently opposed the landowning *hacenderos* on their vast agricultural estates. Now they turned their attention to the invaders, forming the guerrilla organization known as the *Hukbalahap*, a composite name meaning the People's Anti-Japanese Army. In the meantime, the Philippines were being integrated into the new Japanese

empire, the so-called "Great East Asia Co-Prosperity Sphere." The Japanese were claiming that, far from being invaders, they were liberators. Their troops had finally freed the Philippines from the colonial domination of Westerners. Were Filipinos not true Easterners, like the Japanese? Once again, there were many who believed this rhetoric of foreign liberation.

It is safe to say that, of all the traumas Filipinos have collectively undergone since the moment Magellan landed, World War II was by far the worst. In 1945, General MacArthur did return to fight his way back across the archipelago, leaving Manila virtually destroyed, while the last of the Japanese high command surrendered in Baguio. By then, it is probable there remained not a single family anywhere in the country that hadn't known loss, while thousands of families had vanished entirely. And once again, history was about to repeat itself. The postwar world was shaking down into new power blocs. The Hukbalahap, who for years had fought heroically from the inside and who had helped the Americans retake their country from the Japanese, now found themselves labeled as "communist insurgents." Even as full independence was finally granted in 1946, an American-backed military campaign began which aimed at mopping up the guerrillas in the hills who had suddenly turned from being gallant allies into enemies of freedom and democracy.

At the time, there was probably little enough real communist ideology to be found among the ex-Huks, exhausted and decimated as they were by years of jungle living and fighting. Most of them, though, were skeptical about the independence which was finally granted in 1946. Similarly, they regarded the first truly Filipino government of President Roxas as having merely puppet status. Their more avowedly communist successors, the New People's Army, certainly believed the United States was less concerned with Filipino democracy than it was in keeping its military bases and ensuring favorable concessions for American business

GUIDO ALBERTO ROSSI

Historic Corregidor Island's Mile-Long Barracks are hollow ruins left by the Pacific War and they serve as a bleak reminder of the Japanese bombardment of 1941.

interests. They were by no means alone in this view. Many educated Filipinos, including the clergy, who supported the nationalist cause without being remotely communist, came to precisely the same conclusion. And indeed, until the day Corazon Aquino became President in 1986, it was commonly accepted that no Philippine administration had ever taken office without Washington's approval and active connivance.

5

Obviously, anyone may query matters of emphasis in so brief a resume of Philippine history. What cannot be disputed, however, is the relevance of this anguished past to every aspect of today's country. Whether or not the specter of Maoist communism was ever as real as Washington and Manila claimed, when Ferdinand Marcos declared martial law in 1972 he did so with Washington's express approval. This was in order to give himself the extraordinary powers he said he needed to put an end to communist-led subversion. (It was surely not irrelevant to his decision that it empowered him to remain in office indefinitely.) Once more, Filipino guerrillas were hunted bloodily in the hills and once again historic questions were raised. For over eight years the country that had been called "the showcase of democracy" lived under American-supported martial law, with its suppression of habeas corpus and human rights, its electoral fraud, censorship, jailings and torturings. These years between 1972 and 1986 left a deep mark on an already scarred national psyche, a wound which the so-called EDSA Revolution of February 1986 did little to heal. Today, ten years later, many Filipinos argue that the revolt which sent the Marcoses into exile had a parallel with the 1896 Katipunan Revolution, in that both were essentially led by the ilustrado class, and both leaderships sold out their radical element to maintain the status quo. To such critics, the People Power which heroically stopped President Marcos' tanks was more of a middle class revolt led by bankers and liberals.

YANN ARTHUS-BERTRAND

The old questions remained. What was democracy really about? Come to that, what was a Filipino? Who owned the flag to which one's children daily pledged their loyalty at school? Did the chain of command end at the President's desk in Malacañang Palace, or did the buck not stop until it had reached the White House? How could the importance to the United States of its military bases in the Philippines be ignored, both during the Vietnam War and in the larger context of containing communism? In which case, what did Philippine independence mean? Aside from that, was the country really being run in order to make it a better place for the notional common man, Juan de la Cruz, and his wife to bring up their children in peace and freedom?

Even if Juan de la Cruz did not actually voice such questions each day, they formed—and still do—a vital part of his awareness of his country. They arise directly out of a turbulent past, much of which is too recent to be ignored, too painful to be forgotten. Visitors remark on the Filipinos' easygoing cheerfulness, their humor in the face of all sorts of disasters and difficulties, a quality of dogged survival with infinite good grace. These virtues are utterly genuine. Yet from whatever wellspring they flow, they come tinged with a certain pragmatic bleakness. Whether or not it is correct (or even proper) for foreigners to refer to the Philippines as a "damaged culture," it is surely likely that no people could easily reconcile itself to so much betrayal.

Yet somewhere far underneath is an untainted strength, as if Filipinos had only *seemed* to succumb to the blandishments of successive invaders—Spanish, American, Japanese—with their respective pledges of eternal life, eternal democracy and eternal membership of the Great East Asia Co-Prosperity Sphere. This strength recognizes the human values which transcend the merely political. It acknowledges, amid the moral and emotional confusion, that each of the invaders did include among their numbers good and decent people, lovers and lifelong friends, men and women who wished them and the Philippines nothing but well.

A solitary, perfect island of the Sulu Archipelago,
complete with white sand and coral reef.

6

"I enter the future by remembering the past," Rizal once declared. So, with all this in the background (though not forgotten), what will a visitor find in the Philippines of the 1990's? The last American troops have left their old bases. The notorious girlie bars of Subic and Olongapo have all but vanished. A first impression of Manila, though, is still of an externally Americanized culture. Most people speak English, a good number wear jeans and T-shirts, drink Coca-Cola and listen to Western pop music, just as they increasingly do everywhere. But the cautious visitor will beware of falling into the trap of assuming that Manila *is* the Philippines. It isn't. Even a short trip outside the capital reveals a very different country. Coca-Cola can still (but not infallibly) be found in the provinces and people may still wear T-shirts and

ALBERTO 'BULLIT' MARQUEZ

jeans; yet not so much English is spoken, and more and more the land gives off a character uniquely its own.

And the further one travels from Manila, the more this becomes true. Rural life often goes on in ways that have changed surprisingly little since the Spanish left, and which are probably not much different from before they ever came. In the province where I live, produce is still hauled by buffalo along the track from the forest on wooden sleds, and the rice paddies are still plowed by the same buffalo pulling wooden plows. Houses are still built from bamboo and thatch and woven cane, held together by vines and thongs rather than by nails. The coconut palm is still central to the life and economy of many rural areas, supplying not just copra for palm oil but lumber, food, thatch, toddy or palm beer, even clothing material. In an environmentally concerned world, this is no longer taken automatically to be a sign of backwardness. Rather, it represents a way of life perfectly adapted to climate and terrain. Governmental thinking now revolves around how to improve the conditions of people's lives without upsetting this basic harmony. The Philippines is still predominantly agricultural; and this, too, is increasingly seen as a source of strength at a time when the population drift to the cities

throughout Southeast Asia could one day mean crucial shortages in food production.

If the American presence in the Philippines has left its most obvious influence in the governmental system, in the English language and consumer tastes of these islands, the Spanish influence lies somewhat deeper. It pervades the country's spiritual life and customs as well as the national language, Pilipino. The legacy of Spanish Catholicism is at its most obvious in the widespread religious festivals and in the social traditions surrounding birth, death and marriage. Yet the often extreme piety of many Filipinos (famously reflected in the Passion Week and Good Friday pageants each year when a handful of men—and occasionally women—are actually crucified) can be mixed with far more ancient beliefs. It is not unusual to find deeply religious Filipinos with a lively respect for magic, charms, animist spirits, cults, healings and mysteries of all sorts. The official Church may frown, but it makes not a scrap of difference. Having been subjected to so many and varied rulers, the Filipinos have taken their revenge by being spiritually eclectic.

This has a hidden but real relevance to the present, and maybe even to future political developments. It is not just that charismatic healers do a good trade, nor that Chinese Catholics may employ fortune-tellers or *feng shui* experts before building a new office block. Lately, Filipino historians have been uncovering a quite different version of the nineteenth-century revolt against Spain—one that had its roots in peasant movements grouped around magical and charismatic leaders whose objectives were often quite different from the purely liberationist or nationalist ones of the middle class ilustrados. Far from having been directly influenced by Rizal's novels (which most peasants could never have read), it has been suggested that the popular movements which opposed the Spanish, and later the Americans, were inspired by ritual readings of the Biblical account of Christ's Passion; ironically the very text the friars had once used to subjugate Spain's colony.

If true, this is brilliantly perverse and quintessentially Filipino. The secret brotherhoods which formed around these peasant leaders made liberal use of all sorts of symbols and incantations drawn from Christianity, Freemasonry, the occult,

A pig in a cage is driven about in a cab hitched on to a motorbike— just one of the ever-trusty, idiosyncratic vehicles of the provinces.

and folk beliefs. Certain scholars maintain that many of today's charismatic sects are as much popular political movements as they are spiritual. Is history once more repeating itself? Visitors to Manila may well become swept up in one of El Shaddai's huge, fervent rallies, and can decide for themselves.

7

When moving about the country, therefore, the visitor should beware of thinking that the 'guide book' version of the Philippines—the version of the Westernized media and economic experts—is the only one. The true history of the Philippines was always largely unwritten, and so is its present. Appearances to the contrary, the nation's taproot is planted firmly in the Orient. Juan de la Cruz is probably hiding himself quite subtly behind his affability and his cradle-tongue, with a set of beliefs and objectives far less crudely Western than may be imagined.

It is an Eastern pragmatism that has enabled Filipinos to do fascinating things with the cultures foisted on them. At a trivial level, this is apparent in their inventive versions of Chinese, Spanish and Japanese dishes, or in their creation of the jeepney from the jeep. Far more significantly, they have developed complex spiritual and social fabrics which are authentically home-grown. The same historical legacy produces entrepreneurial skills that can deal flexibly with business propositions from outside. Just as well, too; for by a final irony, China and Japan—which a long-dead Spanish king had hoped to conquer spiritually—seem poised for economic supremacy in the region. Those who visit this land thoughtfully will find, not some bland tourist paradise, but a country with a richly unique past, and an even richer future.

PAUL CHESLEY

8

Up until this point I have described the Philippines in general terms. Now I would like to be specific about the part of the Philippines that has become my home but, even though after 16 years it has become unique for me, I know that its diurnal customs, as well as the scenery itself, are echoed in a thousand other rural backwaters throughout the archipelago. It is thus at once unrepeated and commonplace. So let us say that it is late afternoon in the Philippine provinces. Along the track past my hut people are walking up from the village into the woods where they have small plots. The women carry heavy pails of pig-swill on their heads, their barefoot children trot alongside. The little boys often wear the elastic of their catapults around their heads, the leather pouch in the center of their foreheads, the handle dangling down their necks.

One could set an imaginary watch by these comings and goings. They begin at first, gray light when the men walk up to tend their animals and count the chickens down from their roosts in the trees to see if any have fallen prey overnight to the big lizards known as *bayawak* or else to feral cats. At the same time there is a contrary flow; those families from the furthest parts of the village who live in houses along this track among the coconut groves. At about the time when the pig-feeders return, the first children are trotting down to school. Even the smallest and poorest somehow contrive to look neat in clean white shirts and pink dresses. Some miracle as yet unknown in the West will enable them to preserve that pristine appearance even in the rainy season's mud and drenching gusts.

No sooner have the children gone than the first detonations sound from down below in the stream's broad bed beside the track. Their mothers are beginning the day's laundry, squatting together in the shallow water with their skirts hitched up, giving wet heaps of clothes resounding blows from wooden paddles. It is not yet hot. The early sun slants magically between the fronds and branches overhead,

This girl with a million-dollar smile has just been dancing with her father in Rizal Park, Manila.

casting all sorts of golden grilles and lattices through which smoke drifts and insects sparkle. A man tethers his buffalo to a palm trunk downstream from the washers. The animal is on a long rope which ends in a knot through its nose. It lumbers gratefully into the water and finds a deep wallow under the bank where it will later shelter from the day's heat. The bank is severly undercut here, eroded into a hollow by the animal scratching its back. Distinct strata of volcanic pebbles are exposed in the earth.

Before long, the first men arrive to collect the night's seepage of *tuba* or palm wine. Tuba is something of a national drink. It is tapped from the cut flower in the crown of a coconut palm. The sap drips continuously into a bamboo container. It is collected morning and evening and drunk almost immediately since it starts fermenting at once, according to temperature and the yeasts in the container. As the hours pass, tuba becomes more alcoholic as more of the sap's sugars are converted to alcohol, but it also becomes more acrid. Bottled and left to stand, it eventually turns to *suka*, the gentle and distinctive vinegar which gives a characteristic flavor to many dishes. A tuba-gatherer may have to visit half a dozen *karitan*, or toddy-producing palms, twice a day, shinning up and down sheer 60-foot trunks barefoot with a big bamboo container hitched over one shoulder. It is not an easy—or even safe— way to earn a living. But Mando, whom I know well, is clearly cheerful this morning. I can hear him whistling the signature tune of *Villa Quintana*, a popular television soap, up there in the palm crowns while all around him golden orioles and other birds whizz from frond to frond. Down below him the buffalo groans, the women beat and chatter, a cart trundles by. These are the familiar sounds of rural life being lived.

It is impossible not to feel cheered, for there is something reassuring about basic human continuities. Even though in a village like this superficial things are always changing (typhoons and termites deal with trees and houses alike; river banks collapse where buffaloes and currents undermine them) it is in essence a way of life that would readily have been recognizable to someone centuries ago. Some years back we were installing a hand pump down near the river. The diggers had excavated a pit down to about 10 feet when they began throwing out shards of smoke-blackened

BRUNO BARBEY

pottery. At some time in the far-off past other people had decided that this was a good place to live, with fresh water nearby and a forest full of fruit and wood. Immediately, the diggers began hoping for gold or priceless Chinese porcelain. All they got was a view of their own roots, just as we all had a glimpse of our common destiny.

I am thankful that I lived in the Philippine provinces for many years before I came to know Manila. By reversing the usual process I found I had acquired some slight grasp, at least, of a culture and even of a language. It is at this level that the Philippines is both at its most accessible and at its most enigmatically foreign. In due course I was able to recognize in the city's commuter tides and squatter areas many of the rural values and strengths I had already grown to admire. City living conditions are often savage in ways that rural life, no matter how impoverished, is not (even though it is peasants who are supposed to have a monopoly of noble savagery). In any case, as in many other developing countries, a good proportion of the capital's population consists of folk who have migrated, their country habits and attitudes often only thinly overlaid by city ways.

For the last 16 years, then, I have been living in the same provincial *barangay,* and have come to think of it as home. Barangays are administrative divisions—villages by any other name—which hark back to a very distant historical past. Migrating settlers had once set off from what are now Malaysia and Indonesia in enormous boats called barangays, a village to each boat, captained by the headman. Having found an auspicious spot, they landed and more or less set up their old village again. Under the Spanish and Americans the term gradually fell out of use until it was resurrected by the late President Marcos as part of his attempt to generate some collective nationalistic spirit. In fact, barangays represent a highly efficient social system. The captain and his officials are elected at four-yearly intervals. Their village is largely self-policing, with rules for settling minor disputes and the levying of small fines. The community is entitled to an annual allowance of Central Government funds for local projects such as installing water pumps or building a village hall. By and large the system works well; and visitors to the provinces will

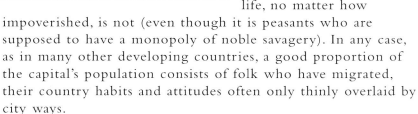

In Zamboanga the Badjaos sell bleached corals like cabbages or flowers.

be impressed by a general feeling of orderliness, as well as by individual differences—in fencing, for instance—that mark off one barangay from its neighbor.

The attentive visitor to Manila will notice that the city, too, is divided into barangays, for nowadays the word has lost its nautical connotations. Yet residually, a sense of the sea permeates even the cities of this archipelago, remaining in the language if scarcely in fact. A young Filipino's circle of friends and allies will constitute a *barkada* or gang, which need not be at all criminal but merely a group which meets to drink or play cards. A barkada, of course, is nothing but the Spanish for 'boatload'. Thus the very words barangay and barkada reinforce the idea of shipmates, of tightly-knit, independent groups of self-sufficient people. This notion is at the very heart of Filipino society, with its elaborately extended families and often narrow regional loyalties. Sometimes this amounts to a downright clannishness which shows as adherence to a particular province or language group. The basis of Pililpino, the national language, is Tagalog— which is the language of the Manila area. The islands known as the

GUEORGUI PINKHASSOV

Visayas in the center of the archipelago have various other languages quite different from Tagalog as well as from those of the Ilocos in the north-west. For this reason many disaffected Tagalogs and Visayans, for example, viewed the 21 years of the Marcos administration as a sort of Ilocano conspiracy, since many of the important cabinet posts and ranks of the Armed Forces were filled with the President's fellow-provincials.

It is interesting how resistant this system is to dilution by mobility. Families split up in search of work, drift to cities, go abroad. Yet everywhere Filipinos meet, they perform brilliant rituals of networking to establish each other's roots, gravitating towards those from the same province. It is almost unimaginable that two fellow-provincials will not discover a name in common. So in Manila, for example, one comes across squatter areas—sometimes entire barrios—whose people all speak Waray, or Ilonggo, or Kapangpangan. Occasionally, barangays can be found that are virtually entire villages

transplanted from a distant province, showing that this old idea of migration still lives on. I find this deeply touching. It means that anyone arriving from that province will be closely questioned for the latest gossip. He will also come bearing grubby, ill-scrawled envelopes from distant relatives, as well as the obligatory *pasalubong*: the presents which may often be no more than some sticky or smelly local delicacy quite unobtainable in Manila which induces a wave of homesick pleasure. So by a system of minor emissaries and chance visitors, a group of Filipinos far from home keep intact a sense of identity.

9

Distance. Separation. Fragmentation. These are the polarities that dominate the lives of so many Filipino families. One might argue that the brutality of world economics underlies many of this country's (and the human race's) most pressing problems. When the full history of migrant workers comes to be written, the Filipinos may well be found to have constituted the single greatest diaspora. There is hardly a snowbound village in Finland, or battered cargo vessel, or Middle-Eastern hospital where they cannot be found. Such a well-trained, willing pool of labor represents a great national economic asset, of course. Yet sometimes one wonders whether certain assets are better kept unexported. Of course, even though there is no denying the value of the remittances such workers send home to their families, it is also true that many do return after their contract is finished with enough money to buy a car and set up as a taxi driver, or to invest in a plot of land and a hog-rearing scheme.

But it seems those who leave this particular barangay must be unlucky in some way, for as yet it has never quite worked out with such copybook precision. People vanish for long stretches, return briefly with a husband or a bride, looking plumper and wearing the correct brand of watch and sunglasses. Then they vanish again, swallowed up in some distant industrial town or in Manila itself. For some reason this village seems only to experience

Coconut palms and park benches, balloons and supertankers line Manila's Roxas Boulevard, famous for great views of great sunsets over Manila Bay.

personal loss without obvious financial compensation.

So at dusk I walk down the track to the village, with the first frogs beginning to croak in the rice paddies. I greet my friends and watch their children playing in the dust between the bamboo huts. In this place they still play singing-and-dancing games, just as they did in Europe earlier this century until the coming of television. The chants and squeals go up into the velvet air while their elders thread their way around the racing children with pails of pig feed.

I listen to these songs which no department of tourism can ever teach, to all the immemorial sounds of a rural life which works so brilliantly on every level except the economic. Many of these are my god-children. It is scarcely bearable to think that someone who once sat on my knee like a little lump of dough, so full of yeasty possibilities, should one day join the great exodus, whether as part of the army of squatters who besiege the capital or as a contract worker abroad. The new United Nations population report says that half of this country's people live in Manila and Cebu. It is best not to dwell on the sort of life that the report says awaits most of those leaving the land. At this time of the evening, with the fireflies and the fruit bats beginning to flutter from the crowns of the palms, I look with special affection on those youngsters one knows will never leave this village. Some of the girls are clearly destined to marry locals and join the other women beating clothes in the river. Certain boys are equally fated to spend their lives climbing palms and plowing, and they are not always those slightly hopeless ones who somehow drift out of school at about 14 and drink too much.

10

While thoughtful visitors to the Philippine provinces can often see all the trappings of a rural idyll, they will not assume it means village life is Edenic. All of it—the slow rituals, the soft moths and children's voices at dusk, the fettling-up of pressure lamps for fishermen to tie on the prows of their little boats—all this is real enough. But it is predicated on a chronic shortage of cash. People do not migrate for fun. They are driven from home. The informed traveler will recognize that the very elements of the scene which suggest that time has stopped (a man plowing a paddy with his buffalo amid the glittering swerve of dragonflies) also say not 'idyll' but 'underdevelopment'. Thousands of accounts from dozens of different cultures the world over tell us that the laborer's life has never been all it was cracked up to be by sentimental townees. The plowman will inform us over a glass of tuba that there's not much he wouldn't prefer to do than wade through knee-deep, glutinous mud for hour after exhausting hour. There are neat little Japanese machines that will do the job quicker and better.

This is not said bitterly or resentfully, but simply stated for the fact it is. No visitor could be disappointed by the mannerly sweetness of these villagers, by their friendliness and generosity and hospitality. Not one of these virtues is a figment of the tourism industry's public relations flacks. They exist as though deliberately to spite any idea that Philippine history might radically have soured the people. Indeed, from time to time I have wondered whether this ability to meet anyone on friendly terms was not an ingenious defensive strategy. Faced over the centuries with so many strangers whose intentions were less than selfless, the Filipino maybe evolved this cunning and disarming ploy. . . . But I don't really believe so. It is more fundamental than that. It seems to stem from an irrepressible optimism.

There is good reason to think that it is a combination of optimism and self-sufficiency which has enabled the Filipino to survive. That, and something I can only describe as a certain *apartness*; the sense that no matter how accurately the blows of fate seem aimed at him, there is always something that remains unhit, as though a part of him were permanently elsewhere. It is a characteristic I have learned to admire and love. Both uncomplaining and faintly amused, it is very un-Western in our debased modern guise, though I suspect it has much in common with the estimable stoicism of our ancestors. No matter what becomes of this planet, it would be no surprise if the last human being left alive on earth turned out to be a Filipino. **J.H-P.**

Two girls try to figure out the best way to take a snapshot of their friends in a playground in Manila.

GUIDO ALBERTO ROSSI

BEAUTY

NATURE,

&

LAND & SEA

BOUNTY

"LIFE-GIVING BREEZES SWEEP THE STRAND"

JOSE RIZAL, FROM *SONG OF MARIA CLARA*

ARTHUR TENG

Previous pages: Pangalusian Island, a white-beach resort from the air. Pangalusian is one of the newest five-star facilities in the El Nido family of beach resorts, located amid the natural environment of northern Palawan.

Above: Children play in the clear waters of Boracay.

Opposite: An aerial view of Luzon gives the land the look of an abstract painting.

Long, long ago, there were only the sky and the sea and a solitary bird that flew endlessly between them, for there was no place in the sky or on the sea where it could rest. The bird cunningly provoked a quarrel between the sky and the sea. The sea stormed the sky with its mighty waves. The sky rose higher and threw down a great number of rocks, subduing the sea and creating a multitude of islands.

The bird, pleased by the outcome, found a place to rest. Then a bamboo trunk washed ashore and struck the feet of the bird. The bird pecked it and split it open. From the hollow of one node came the first man, and from the hollow of the next node came the first woman. The man and woman became husband and wife and from their union came numerous children.

This, according to an ancient legend, is how the Philippines was formed and inhabited.

As you may imagine, science and history tell a different tale. The islands are the tops of mountains that rise from the sea. They were formed millions of years ago by the uplift, folding and cracking of the sea floor, the swelling of molten rock towards the surface and the eruption of volcanoes. Parts of the larger islands, which are now fertile land, were once under water. There are about 100 volcanoes in the islands of the Philippines, 20 of them active, and 80 dormant or extinct. A number of them reign magnificently over the horizon, reminding the land of its origins.

Lying 1,000 kilometers off the coast of Asia, and spread north to south over 1,500,000 square kilometers of territorial waters, the 7,107 islands of the Philippines cover a land area of 300,000 square kilometers. Forty-five islands have an area of 100 square kilometers or more. The rest are smaller islands, islets and rocks. About 3,000 islands are named. A large, though undetermined number, are uninhabited. For all the density of its urban areas, the volume of overseas trade and travel, and the omnipresence of modern technology, the country is still a beautiful paradise of desert isles.

The Hundred Islands, which are in fact several hundred islands, are a mini-archipelago in the Lingayen Gulf. The islands appear to have been a coral reef that was once covered by lava from a nearby volcano, then shattered into separate islands by a violent eruption. Flying over the country one sees the larger islands, their satellites, and isolated islets enjoying absolute privacy.

Writers, even scholarly ones, cannot resist the temptation to describe the archipelago as a string of emeralds. The lush vegetation, flooded with the brilliant light of day or shadowy in the soft light of sunset, excites the romantic imagination. Tropical foliage has a wide spectrum of shades of green, ranging from light yellowish, cheerful green, through tender, succulent green, to deep, somber, mysterious green. The spectrum becomes even wider when one sees sunlight playfully filtering through leafy screens and canopies. In the refreshing density of tropical vegetation, one imagines how the world looked at the time of creation. Or how lovely the primal wilderness was before human beings came into it.

When were these islands inhabited? Stone tools found in the northern part of Luzon indicate that human beings lived here 400,000 to 500,000 years ago. However, the earliest human remains, found in the Tabon caves on the island of Palawan, go back to around 22,000 B.C. There have been various theories on how the islands came to be inhabited. The oldest, and most romantic of them, proposes that migrants came in waves, bravely crossing the seas, and discovered this virgin land. But this idea has been discounted by scholars who say that the waves were mere trickles and others who say that human beings had already been in the islands of Southeast Asia for more than a million years.

By about A.D. 1000, the islanders were engaged in commerce with traders from China, Indo-China, the Malay Archipelago, India and Arabia. When Ferdinand Magellan came to the Philippines in 1521, he found villages and what his chronicler called "a city" and people who were willing to embrace Christianity. In 1565, the islands became a colony of Spain. By the end of Spanish rule in 1898, the population, largely Christian then, was about seven million.

Today the Philippines is home to almost 70 million people. Almost half of them are 20 years old and younger. There are 78 ethnolinguistic groups, of which two account for more than 50% of the population, and the next six for about 35%. Thirty-three of the groups are further divided into a total of 153 subgroups. What these figures show is not only the multiplicity of languages and dialects, but also the amazing variety and richness of our culture.

A visitor who traverses the entire length of the country, from the sparsely populated Batanes Islands in the north to the colorful Tawi-Tawi Archipelago in the south, encounters the fascinating, if not bewildering, diversity of Philippine language, music, dance, architecture, traditional attire, cuisine and handicrafts. Charmed by the gentleness, warmth and humor of the population everywhere, one is reminded that the Philippines is one country and one people.

As one explores the islands, one sees how people learn to live joyfully with nature and succeed in creating a setting of beauty for their lives. In the rugged terrain of the Cordillera in northern Luzon, the Ifugao, Bontoc and Kalinga have built terraces on the mountainsides so that rice plants can grow in well-watered paddies. The majestic rice terraces of Banaue are 2,000 years old and are still cultivated. In the south, where the water around islands is calm yet constantly flowing, the Samal build their houses on stilts over the water, to cool the rooms. The boat is not only a means of livelihood and transport but can also be an emblem of joy. The Tausug *vinta*, with its strikingly designed and brightly-colored sail, is a sight that lifts the spirit. For the Badjao, who are sea gypsies, the boat is home and land is only visited when buying rice and burying the dead.

In the beautiful hilly region around Lake Sebu in south Cotabato, the T'boli build their houses on hilltops—preferably one house to a hilltop. Lakeshore dwellers all over the country build traps to catch fish, or pens in which to raise them. An active volcano is not always a threat to life, but is always admired as a thing of beauty, so people live and work in its shadow.

Rice fields and rice terraces, fish ponds and fish pens, villages and cities, highways and bridges tell of a people's impact on the land. Yet in many places in these islands—forests and mountain tops, seashores and coral reefs—nature remains untouched and unspoiled. Sunlight, wind, rain and the cycle of seasons are all part of the gift and spirit of nature which no man can alter. As people unceasingly labor to change the landscape, one wonders how the land in turn has fashioned their character and soul.

R.D.P.

Previous pages: Fishpens divide up magnificent Lake Sebu in South Cotabato, Mindanao. This picturesque lake is the ancient homeland of the T'boli people, an animist hilltribe recognized by their elaborate costumes of ikat cloth, beads and brass anklets.
BRUNO BARBEY

BRUNO BARBEY

Like Magritte's giant fish in the sky, two fresh tuna are unloaded by a muscled fisherman on the beach of General Santos City, southern Mindanao. Most of the tuna caught in the seas of Sarangani Bay are bound for the tables of Japan where the ordinary seafood bounty of Philippine waters is deemed gourmet fare.

PRESCIANO (SONNY) YABAO

A serene moment in time sits anchored by Bohol Island. Fishing vessels off the pier of Tagbilaran cross watery paths with motor yachts under the brilliant blue skies. Boat boys gather seawater to keep their catch sea-fresh, while the island province of Bohol contemplates which direction to take her ancient cultural heritage and her new scuba-diving tourists.

Two men contemplate the day during a moment of quiet. Fighting the waves to catch food for their families and gather produce for the market is just part of the routine for the people of Camiguin Island.

Following pages: A solitary boat drifts through Sitangkai, the 'Venice of the East.'

A time to wash, a time to bathe, in the waters of Mindanao.
About four million Muslims live in the southernmost
Philippine island, mostly in Lanao and Cotabato. The major
Muslim groups live in organized societies oriented toward the
Muslim cultures of neighboring Indonesia, Malaysia
and Brunei.

A boy born on the sea flips himself off the deck to cool off
in the waters of homeland Zamboanga. Zamboanga City,
known as the City of Flowers, was the capital of Mindanao
for over 300 years. As early as the thirteenth and fourteenth
centuries, Zamboanga was a barter trade center for the
Chinese, Malay and other seafaring peoples of the Southeast
Asian region.

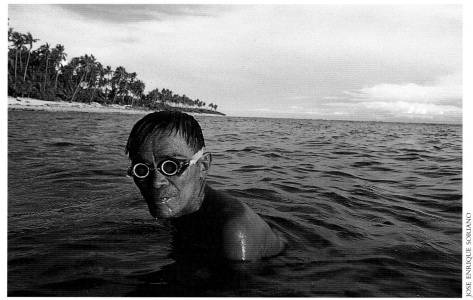

JOSE ENRIQUE SORIANO

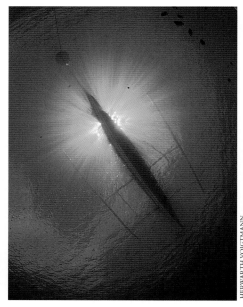

HERWARTH VOIGTMANN

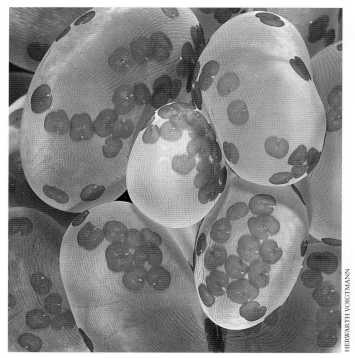

HERWARTH VOIGTMANN

YANN ARTHUS-BERTRAND

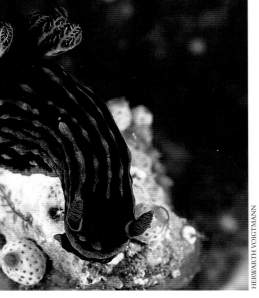

The Philippine Archipelago is a unique island ecosystem with the widest variety of marine species in the world—up to 2,000 varieties of fish and 500 of coral. In tropical seas or inland lakes, water temperatures average 25°-31°C. These warm waters with strong currents are ideal for corals to grow, fish to spawn, cuttlefish to mate, and scuba divers to enjoy the unparalleled bounty of the marine underworld.

*M*alapacao Island in the El Nido island group is a safe port of call for fishing boats and sailing yachts around Bacuit Bay, northern Palawan. Towering granite cliffs and a cove with calm waters surround a rustic resort with its pier reaching outwards. Marina del Nido is well-equipped to service yachts and other vessels which drift in from the seas.

*T*he Manila Southwoods golf course in Carmona, Cavite (above and right), comprises an enormous 430-hectare golf community—a most ambitious project of Fil-Estate Land, Inc., the innovative developer. The two courses, The Masters and The Legends, were planned by golf professional Jack Nicklaus and are built to the highest standards.

They call it a marine paradise, this wondrous place called El Nido. The clearest seas for snorkeling, scuba-diving and just taking in the awesome natural environment are in the El Nido marine reserve on the north end of Palawan.

Northern Palawan's marine environment comprises bays and lagoons amongst limestone isles—replete with caves and marine gardens, rain forests and rocky cliffs. In the past decade, hoteliers have discovered northern Palawan and have quickly claimed islands to build boutique resorts upon.

Following pages: A seaborne tapestry of fish cages and seaweed plots sways upon the currents of the Sulu Seas. Long grid contraptions are floated offshore, and the marine produce is gathered by the community on the shore.

YANN ARTHUS-BERTRAND

YANN ARTHUS-BERTRAND

*T*he crater of Mount Pinatubo (above), the volcano that has wreaked havoc and destruction on Luzon since June 1991. Bohol, the oval-shaped island province of the Visayas (right) is known for its verdant lands, deep waters, and the natural and cultural sites of scuba-diving and ancient churches.

The numerous 'haycock' hills (right)—known as the Chocolate Hills—are Bohol's premier natural attraction.

PRESCIANO (SONNY) YABAO

The awesome Pantabangan dam in the Sierra Madre highlands of Nueva Ecija Province (above.) The Upper Pampanga River Project in Pantabangan is a great engineering feat which controls and directs the river's water to supply the rice-growing Central Plain—especially land-locked Nueva Ecija—with vital water and power. The Agno River (left) winds across rice fields in Pangasinan, northern Luzon.

Mount Pinatubo's eruption in June 1991 was the most devastating volcanic explosion of the century. Half a million people were displaced by the ash that rained down and later by the lahar (mudflows) that destroyed 87,000 hectares of the Central Plain and continues to plague the area during rainy season. Today vehicles creep across the gray landscape and residents continue to dig out their properties from the lahar.

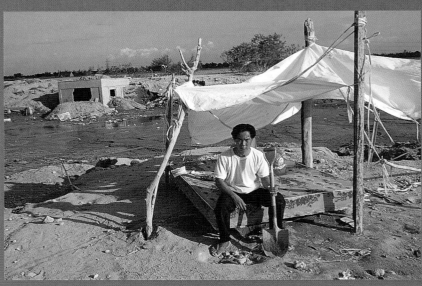

Under the gaze of Mount Mayon, the Bicolanos of Albay work—with the volcano looking over their shoulders. Mayon Volcano last exploded in February 1993, after erupting more than a dozen times this century. Beautiful but deadly, Mount Mayon dominates the province visually, geographically, historically, culturally and economically.

The pineapple, a spiky fruit grown in southern Mindanao, gave its town environs its first name—Dadiangas, meaning 'thorny shrub'. In 1939 pioneers led by General Paulino Santos established a city, General Santos City, on Sarangani Bay. Today, the city has about 250,000 inhabitants and a most productive hacienda, the Dole plantation.

The cane harvest catches the early morning light in the fields of Bacolod, Negros, prime sugar country of the Visayas. On and off the cane plantations the Negrenses' prosperity is reliant on sugar prices. Five years after the drop in the world price of sugar, Bacolod has finally returned to the hacienda lifestyle of the nineteenth century.

MICHAEL FREEMAN

EMIL DAVOCOL

Recently introduced as a commercial enterprise, rubber is now a major industry of Makilala, south of Kidapawan, north Cotabato. In alternate groups, every few hours, the workers tap and gather the sticky white liquid from the rubber trees. This raw material is collected, processed and turned into the tires of big industry by the international rubber companies, Goodyear and Firestone, based in Mindanao.

"Planting rice is never fun," goes the popular rhyme, *"bent from morn till the set of sun."* These farmers of northern Samar prepare the field (above) and then painstakingly plant the rice seedlings (below right).

*T*his vegetable carrier of Ifugao (left, top) pauses on the trail to Batad in the Cordillera Mountains. The two images in the center show the 2,000-year-old stone rice terraces that surround his village. The view of Mindanao (bottom) shows the farmers' geometric plots.

PETER KORNISS

This Kalinga woman with her pipe and rice grain 'hat' lives in Bugnay Village in the northeastern Cordilleras. Isolated because of geography, the Kalinga people were once headhunters but, in these more peaceful days, they excel in story-telling and tribal dancing.

JEAN-PAUL FERRERO

RIO HELMI

ARTHUR TENG

JEAN-PAUL FERRERO

JEAN-PAUL FERRERO

JEAN-PAUL FERRERO

PRESCIANO (SONNY) YABAO

KARL AMMANN

KARL AMMANN

Among the 233 species of Philippine animals, the rare species include: the Palawan bearcat (opposite, top); the Calamian Deer (opposite, middle right); the Mouse Deer (opposite, bottom right): the tarsier, a tiny nocturnal, carnivorous monkey (this page, left top); and the Haribon (this page, right top, from Hari ng Ibon, king of the birds,), the eagle that is endangered but is being raised in the Mount Apo Center in its rain forest environment.

JEAN–PAUL FERRERO

RIO HELMI

JEAN–PAUL FERRERO

Recently introduced giraffes and zebras live on Calauit Island, Palawan, on a wildlife reserve that resembles a savannah.

Following pages: A garden of cock-coops high on a hill. The triangular shade sheds are home for the fighting cocks on this breeding farm in La Paz, Zamboanga.
BRUNO BARBEY

LEONG KA TAI

CHAPTER
TWO

SOUL &
RELIGION

HISTORY
& TRADITION

"TO MY CREATOR I SING"

GUEORGUI PINKHASSOV

Previous pages: The retablo or altar wall of the Binondo Church in Manila sports carved saints and an image of the first Filipino saint, San Lorenzo Ruiz (seen above the heads of the three priests).

Above: Church-inspired buildings abound all over the Philippines, as in this school in Manila.

Opposite: A church in Leyte catches the evening light.

With its neo-Baroque façade and dome, Quiapo Church is an anachronism in twentieth-century Manila. Along its eastern wall roars the heavy traffic of Quezon Boulevard. A few blocks to the west, the elevated Light Railway Transit rumbles over Rizal Avenue. To the south, across a confusion of buildings, is the bustling Pasig River. In the district of Quiapo and its vicinity are populous downtown universities, sprawling markets, enormous department stores, decrepit movie houses, crowded shops and restaurants and buildings in various stages of construction, renovation and decay.

Amid the hubbub, but not overwhelmed by it, stands the church, formally called the Basilica of the Black Nazarene. Within it is another world, a quiet world, though just as crowded with the interminable traffic of devotees. Enshrined at the main altar is an image of Christ in a purple robe carrying the cross. The image, said to be miraculous, came from Mexico in the early seventeenth century. In a small chapel beside the entrance is a copy of the same image which is used for processions. On the left, as one enters, is the crucified Christ, and on the right, in a glass case, is the dead Christ in a purple shroud.

Devotees line up behind the main altar and at the other shrines to kiss or wipe the feet of the image. In the pews men and women, young and old, pray the rosary or a novena or sit quietly meditating and resting. In the middle aisle, devotees walk on their knees slowly towards the altar as they pray. Some devotees are dressed in purple, like the Black Nazarene, in fulfillment of a vow. At the portal of the church are beggars, invalids, healers, fortune-tellers and old women who pray the rosary for a fee. Outside the church are vendors selling religious images, medals, scapulars, rosaries, tapers, amulets and herbs. The church is crowded daily but especially on Fridays and is packed to overflowing on January 9th, the day of the district fiesta, and on Monday of Holy Week, when devotees and pilgrims from all over the country come for a mammoth procession.

Across Quezon Boulevard, screened by buildings and houses, is a stately mosque with a golden dome. The Muslim community that lives around it gathers there to pray, especially on Fridays. At the hours of prayer, the muezzin's call is heard, floating sinuously above the secular sounds of the district.

Quiapo is an icon of faith in the Philippines. It shows the Filipino observing traditions that conform with universal belief and practice, as well as traditions that are of folk origin. More than that, Quiapo shows how faith has prevailed in an increasingly faithless world. Yes, people still believe in God and in the efficacy of prayer. If they are overcome by the weakness of human nature, they believe in the inexhaustible mercy of a forgiving God.

In Quiapo Church, faith takes on a penitential mood as one worships the suffering Christ. But faith can be joyful as on Christmas and Easter, or quiet and prayerful, trusting and confident, as one expresses it in everyday life. Whatever its mood, faith is alive in the Philippines and has always been alive.

Centuries before Islam and Christianity came to these islands, the people had their own religion. They believed in a supreme deity and in lesser divinities. The Tagalog called their god *Bathala*; the Bisaya of Panay called him *Kaptan*; the Bisaya of Occidental Negros called him *Laon*. To this day the people of the Cordillera call him *Kabuniyan*; the Manuvu call him *Manama*; the Bagobo call him *Pamulak Manobo*. The peoples of the Philippines have always had myths about creation, the peopling of the earth, and the flood. They believed in the afterlife, but not in hell. Their world abounded with spirits—ancestor spirits, nature spirits and guardian spirits. Anthropologists say that the early Filipinos' belief in a supreme god, lesser deities and intercessory spirits disposed them to embrace Christianity with its one transcendent God and the celestial community of angels and saints.

The first Muslim missionary came to Sulu, in the south, around 1380, but Islam became widespread in Mindanao after its establishment in Cotabato in 1475. By the sixteenth century, Islam had spread

ROMEO GACAD

to some of the other islands. Manila was a Muslim kingdom when it was conquered by Spanish forces in 1571.

When Ferdinand Magellan explored these islands in 1521, he tried to implant the Christian faith. He himself preached some basic doctrines of Christianity to the people with the help of a native interpreter. The chronicle of his voyage mentions that in Cebu 800 men, women and children were baptized. The wife of the king of Cebu was given an image of the Holy Child when she was baptized. The initial missionary efforts quickly ended, for Magellan was killed in a battle in Mactan, and his men left the islands.

When Miguel Lopez de Legazpi and his troops occupied Cebu in 1565, a soldier found a box with the image of the Holy Child in an abandoned house, probably the same one Magellan had given to the king's wife in 1521. The image is now enshrined in the Basilica of the Santo Niño in Cebu and is the object of widespread devotion.

The chief concern of Spain was to Christianize and govern the people, although the Spaniards also began their search for gold. The work of evangelizing was undertaken by the Augustinians, the Jesuits, the Franciscans, the Dominicans and the Recollects. Towns were organized to facilitate the preaching of the gospel, as well as to strengthen Spanish rule. Churches were built in all the towns, and chapels in the villages. When Spain ceded the Philippines to the United States in 1898, it was a largely a Christian country.

Today about 83% of the Filipino population are Roman Catholic; 5.43% are Protestant; 4.47% are Muslim; and 2.63% belong to the Iglesia ni Cristo. In caves on the slopes of Mount Banahaw there are a number of cults whose doctrine and rituals appear to be borrowings from diverse religions. Catholicism has been revitalized by the charismatic movement, while fundamentalists form their fellowship groups.

Faith is not only practised but celebrated, with piety and solemnity, with joy and exuberance, as it pervades the life cycle, from birth through growth, marriage, old age, to death as to the passage to eternity. Every year is a cycle of celebrations. Christians celebrate Advent, Christmas and the Epiphany, Lent, Passion Week and Easter, recalling the life of Christ and rejoicing in the mystery of redemption. Aside from these, there are the feasts of the Blessed Virgin throughout the year, and the feasts of the patron saints of towns and villages. On November 1st, All Saints Day, cemeteries are crowded as people honor the dead, lighting candles and adorning the tombs with flowers. Muslims celebrate the Islamic New Year, Ashura, Hari-Raya Poasa marking the end of Ramadan, and Hari-Raya Hajj, which commemorates Abraham's willingness to sacrifice his son at God's command.

Throughout the year and throughout the country, in cities and villages, one sees faith, binding people together in belief and prayer, as a source of strength and joy. **R.D.P.**

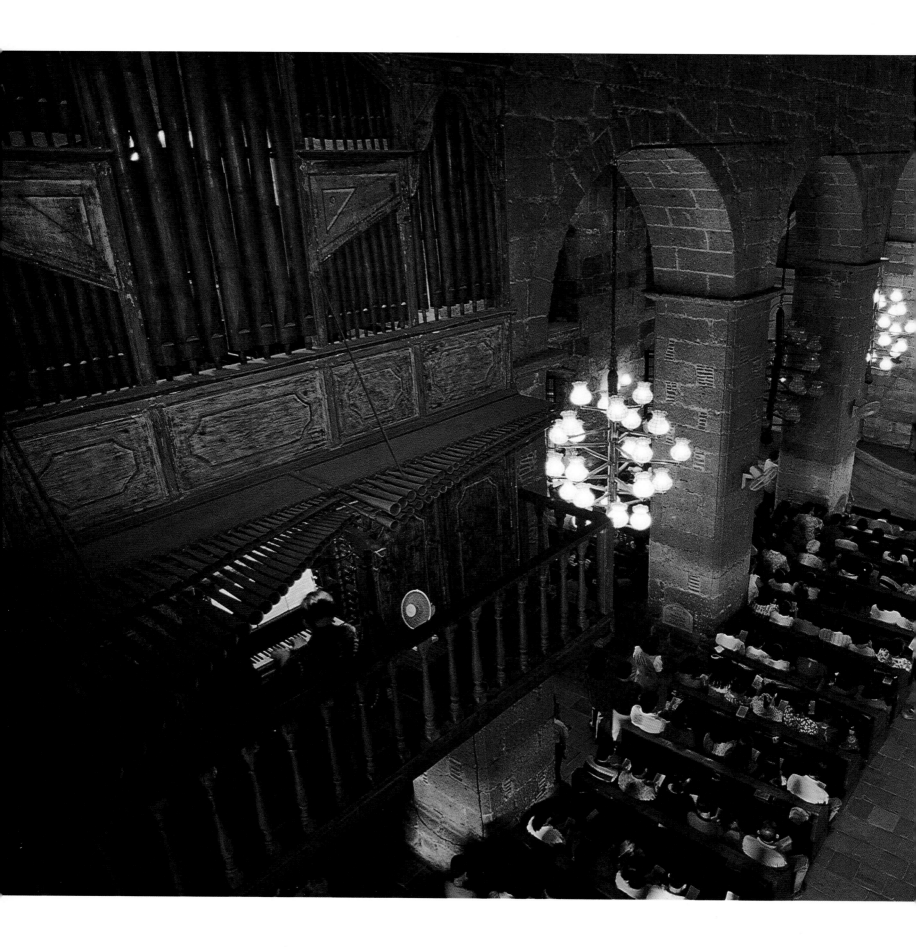

RIO HELMI

Previous pages: Cardinal Jaime Sin, Archbishop of Manila, enjoys a laugh with two religious sisters. In Sin, the Philippines has an irrepressible church leader who is outspoken, involved and recognized as an opinion-maker. In 1986 Sin played a pivotal role in the EDSA Revolution.
CATHERINE KARNOW

Altar boys prepare for the Mass in the Santa Maria Church in Ilocos Sur. The church is an imposing old edifice made with fine red bricks, heavy rounded columns, decorative reliefs and abbreviated buttresses—situated high upon a windy hill that looks out to sea. Reached by a grand staircase, the church has been placed on the Unesco World Heritage list of buildings to be preserved.

The Las Piñas Church, with its elegant bamboo and capiz interiors, is a fitting showcase for the unique Bamboo Organ. The four-meter wide musical instrument, built in 1795 by Father Diego Cera and rediscovered in 1911, has 174 bamboo pipes and 122 horizontal reeds of soft metal. Every February the Bamboo Organ Festival features a repertoire of concert music.

*L*ight a votive candle—in memory of a loved one or just to gain blessings while in church. People all around the Philippines gravitate toward the church for the important events of life; baptisms, weddings, death. In modern times old church rituals still punctuate people's daily lives and religious rites mark the different stages of life.

The Basilica of the Santo Niño in Cebu contains the first santo (wooden saint) to be brought to the Philippines. The 30-centimeter wooden statue of the Christchild was gifted by Magellan to Queen Juliana in 1521, then was lost for many years. It was rediscovered in 1565, after a fire set by Miguel Lopez de Legaspi. The Santo Niño was found unscathed— and was declared miraculous.

LEONG KA TAI

A wedding ends with a rain of ticker-tape—instead of the traditional rice grains— at the San Agustin Church in Intramuros. Being the ancient and favorite church for saying vows, San Agustin does constant business officiating at wedding nuptials, providing uniformed attendants, choir singers and electric organs. On weekends, the familiar "Here comes the bride" plays every hour on the hour.

EDWIN TUVAY

Baptism in the name of the Father and of the Son . . . Baptism into the Roman Catholic faith is the first ritual sacrament performed upon a month-old infant and is a cause for celebration. The Spanish colonization of the archipelago from the sixteenth century has left a legacy of rituals (right), churches and clergy.

PAUL CHESLEY

EDWIN TUYAY

PAUL CHESLEY

*L*ife and death in Manila. The baptism (above) of a Japino (the term Japino is derived from the union of a Japanese and a Filipino parent). Anne Marie Lacson was a former musical entertainer in Japan—where she married her employer, a local businessman. The death (left) of twenty-year-old jeepney driver, Cesar A. Desumala.

Evening light animates the architecture of the Philippines. A stained glass window throws a pool of color onto the flag-stones of a neighborhood church in Bohol (left), and the day's fading sunlight warms the upper story of a house in Vigan.

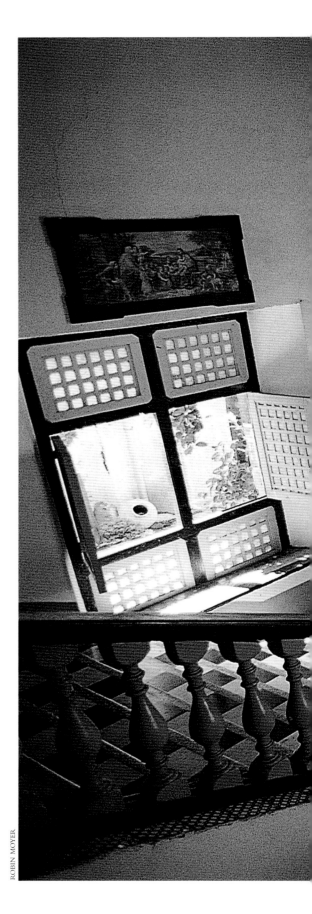

DOMINIC SANSONI

ROBIN MOYER

Carmina Villaroel, an actress in a turn-of-the-century mestiza dress, poses by a capiz shell window in the perfect period location of Vigan, Ilocos Sur. The town of Vigan is so redolent of history, with its stone houses standing shoulder to shoulder over narrow streets, that a viewer is immediately transported back to a bygone age.

The religious inherit the finest buildings. The Holy Rosary Minor Seminary in Naga City, Albay, Bicol, runs classes and holds prayers in its 200-year-old religious institution. Seminarians walk on antique tiles and study to be priests in a period library. Naga is a friendly town of Bicolandia, most famous for its spectacular Peñafrancia Festival on the river— and pili nuts in all their confections.

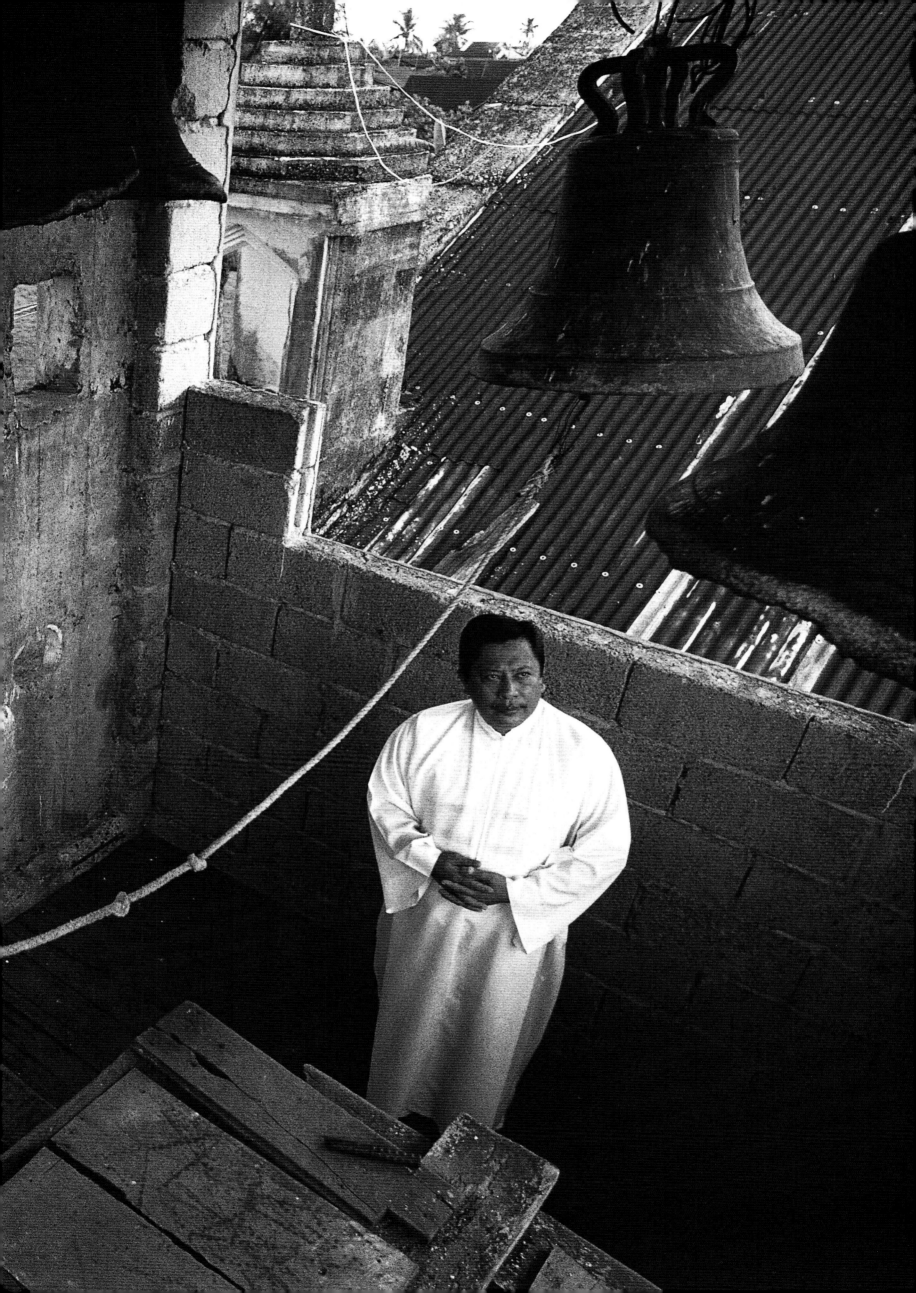

The statue of Father Jose Burgos stands tall against the cloudy sky. This is a portion of the evocative Gomburza Monument by Filipino modernist sculptor Solomon Saprid. The entire work, made of welded brass sheets, is located near Intramuros, reminding citizens of the three priests, Gomez, Burgos and Zamora, who first defied the Spanish word in 1872 and were garrotted as martyrs.

Sweeping up the hallowed hall of the Monsignors. The San Agustin Museum alongside the ancient church echoes with the many Masses, prayers and wedding marches that sing through the grand adobe hallways. The Augustinian Church stands in Intramuros—the walled city built by the Spanish from 1591 to 1785—surviving as the country's oldest church, after war, fire and time itself.

*C*arving the Christ in Paete, Laguna. Woodcarving has always been synonymous with Paete, whose name denotes the people who are expert in using the chisel or paet. Encouraged by the Spanish to try their chisels at religious statuary, Paetenos have carved crucifixes and church pulpits for the world. They also carve statues and reliefs of country life, wooden toys, and fancy bakya *(wooden clogs)*.

The Iglesia ni Cristo is one of the most dynamic contemporary religious movements in Asia with adherents in 73 countries. This Church was first preached in Manila in 1914 by the late Brother Felix Y. Manalo. Today the Iglesia maintains numerous modern Gothic worship buildings that are landmarks throughout the Philippines. Shown above is the Church's Central Temple in Quezon City.

Evening light paints an ethereal view of the Vigan cemetery on a hillock, seen from the Bantay church tower—an apt scene introducing Vigan, the oldest heritage town of the Philippines. Vigan, Ilocos Sur, is an intact eighteenth-century town, complete with giant bahay na bato (houses of stone) that have stood for centuries, unscathed.

'*El Shaddai*' *is a phenomenon of religious enthusiasm. Every Saturday night on a stage on Roxas Boulevard, the charismatic prayer-leader Mike Velarde (above) moves the masses to sing and dance together in praise of the Lord. Thousands wave their hands in prayer. The policeman in uniform and the matron all sing Hallelujah. And the media are there taking it all in.*

DOMINIC SANSONI

The Santo Niño-seller in shades promises a buyer good luck. The popular cult around the Santo Niño—Christ as a child—started in Cebu, but has been embraced by Filipinos everywhere. During the holy infant's feast in January, Santo Niño followers display their personal Niños, dressed in beautiful clothes or in the attire of their doting owner's occupation.

RIO HELMI

The Philippines is a country rich with religion—over 85% of the population are Christians. Catholics in Manila sit line upon line as young and old meet to pray in Southeast Asia's only Christian country.

*M*uslims in Zamboanga kneel towards Mecca to pray, the call of the Imam still sounding in their ears. The region's four million followers of Islam form the majority in only four provinces—out of 70.

Three boys play with their prayer beads during their religious instruction in the local mosque. The call to prayer is heard gently drifting over the beautiful landscape of the southern Philippines five times daily.

Worship in a Muslim village in Zamboanga. While Muslims today constitute a 9% cultural minority of the population, in the mid-1500's Muslims formed the ruling class of traders and missionaries in Luzon. They were in command in Maynila, an outpost of the Bornean and Sulu sultanates.

*H*ealing amid the rocks, fire and water. Brother Luther Villafane, 45, a faith healer, is the leader of one of the many religious sects to be found on Mount Banahaw, the holy mountain between southern Laguna and Quezon. Considered a spiritual place where the healing power of nature is channeled, Mount Banahaw harbors many folk sects, which are basically Catholic, sprinkled with mysticism and animism.

The skulls of carabao and pigs outside this Ifugao hut signify the offerings made by the family to please the gods of Kabunian, the Ifugao heaven. The life of the Ifugao is full of ceremonies; a pig is killed to consult the word of the spirits; and tapuy, *the rice wine, is always drunk as libation with the gods.*

Following pages: A sidewalk faith healer treats a patient's arm with herbal concoctions, oils and incantations. The act of curing simply by prayer or by touch without the aid of implements or drugs empowers the local faith healer or herb doctor. Faith healers claim to be guided by Christian deities but they may have a measure of medical know-how.
CATHERINE KARNOW

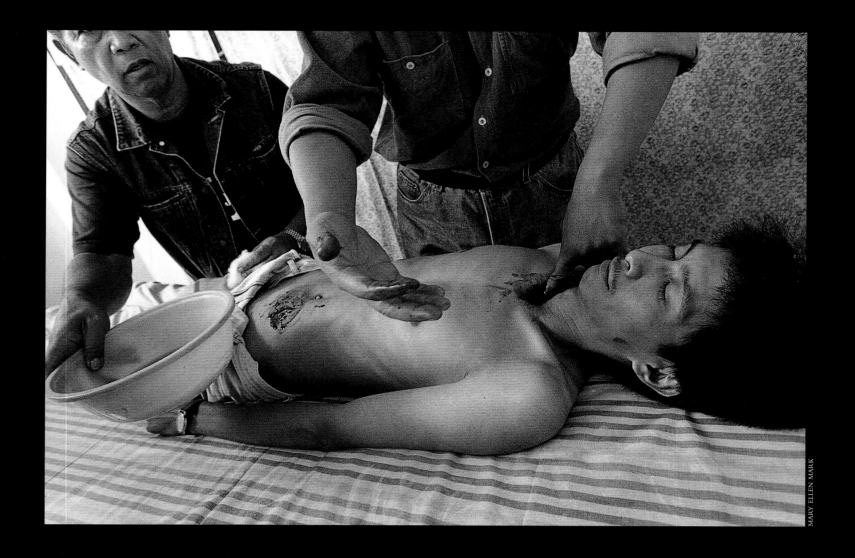

*C*hildren mourn in a funeral parlor in Tondo. Tondo is one of the most impoverished areas in Manila. Out of the estimated 1.5 million people living in this area, more than half are under 20 years of age.

*F*aith healer Brother Joseph Calano and Brother Richard Casuga heal patient Reuen Guerrero of Baguio City. The healers open up bodies and extract diseased parts— without the use of anesthesia or surgical instruments.

*L*ife-size figures of Mary, Joseph, Jesus and the angel from
a shrine outside Bacolod City. Small figurines of La Sagrada
Familia, *the Holy Family, are commonly kept inside the
home, signifying harmony and blessings for the family.
This large group, arranged outdoors on church premises,
prays in silence—while they await their annual role in
the Christmas pageant.*

The first woman President, Corazon C. Aquino (1986-92), is circled by her sisters in contemplation, the Pink Sisters. During the first days of the EDSA Revolution (February, 1986), Mrs. Aquino sought refuge in a Carmelite convent. She rose like a phoenix from the ashes of martial rule to lead the country in the name of her assassinated husband, Ninoy Aquino.

CATHERINE KARNOW

*F*ormer President (1961-65) and Mrs. Diosdado Macapagal. Macapagal, fifth President of the Republic, once claimed he had visited every barrio in the Philippines. He is best known for removing import controls; writing the Land Reform Bill; and changing the date of Independence—from the American-designated event of July 4th, 1945, to the first Filipino Proclamation of Independence on June 12th, 1898.

*I*melda R. Marcos, former First Lady, poses in an embroidered terno *(national dress)* in her apartment overlooking Makati. She and her husband were removed from office in February 1986; they lived in exile in Hawaii, where Ferdinand Marcos died in 1989. In 1995 Imelda Marcos re-entered politics and was elected Congresswoman for Leyte Province.

CATHERINE KARNOW

*T*he Philippine Military Academy in Baguio City is the oldest military college in Asia and the most difficult school to get into. The Academy trains only 1,000 outstanding cadets for the military. Plebes at the mess (above) eat with straight backs, without looking at their food; while cadets practise fencing (left, bottom), PMA's strongest sport. Every Saturday the entire corps dons full dress uniform for the parade review.

Following pages: It's the early morning flag-raising ceremony in the biggest high school in the world. The Rizal High School in Pasig City, Metro Manila, has 19,703 students—making it the biggest secondary school in the world in terms of enrolment. Such is the evidence of the 2.2% annual birth rate of the Philippines.
EDWIN TUYAY

CHAPTER
THREE

LIFE'S

CITY &

WORK

COUNTRY

CHAPTER THREE

"FOR THE INDUSTRY OF A MAN SUSTAINS THE NATION"

JOSE RIZAL, FROM *HYMN TO LABOR*

PRESCIANO (SONNY) YABAO

Previous pages: The Pasig River by Jones Bridge, Manila. Cargo boats chug through the mouth of the 16-kilometer river that spills into Manila Bay.
Above: Happy working the rice in Bohol.
Opposite: Fishermen haul in their nets at the end of a long day.

The cock crows in the darkness of early morning not only in the countryside but also in the crowded neighborhoods of the city. Even before its reveille, many are astir: fishermen who expect a good catch on a moonless night; farmers who want to reach their distant fields before sunrise; jeepney drivers who serve early morning commuters; market vendors who have to prepare their stalls; office workers who religiously avoid the rush hour; and students who have a mortal fear of being marked as being tardy. While the day begins for most people, it ends for some; the night shift at hospitals, 24-hour stores, all-night restaurants, and construction projects, and the taxicab drivers who work 24 hours straight every other day.

As the dark sky gently brightens and the sun emerges with lordly splendor from the horizon, country and city are fully awake. The streets and highways are gradually flooded with vehicles of all shapes and sizes—pushcarts, bicycles, pedicabs, horse-drawn rigs, jeepneys, cars, taxicabs, delivery vans and buses—while sidewalks begin to overflow with people—students in their school uniforms, housewives in plain dresses, office workers in smart attire, laborers in working clothes. The better dressed—professionals, executives and government officials—are in airconditioned cars. Public vehicles are filled to maximum capacity; private cars are sparsely occupied.

The day begins, but its rhythm varies from place to place. It is slow in farms and fishing villages. After the rice seedlings have been planted in the paddies, what else can one do but let them grow and bear their clusters of grain? When fish have been caught, what else can one do but wait until the next propitious time for fishing? In mountain hamlets and in villages by the sea, women weave richly hued textiles following ancient patterns of stylized symbols. Colorful mats and sturdy baskets are skillfully woven; wood is deftly carved into images or implements; red clay pots are expertly shaped, and all this is done with the patience needed to produce art.

The pace of life is faster in the clutch of cities called Metro Manila and the scale of activity is staggering. Armies of workers troop daily to factories and construction sites and vast legions of office workers man the great fortresses of trade and finance. Young men and women, boys and girls, hurrying or cheerfully chattering, swarm in and occupy the universities and schools. The old wet markets and the new Western-style supermarkets, shopping malls and department stores welcome the daily invasion of customers, from housewives shopping alone to entire families on a buying expedition, eager to carry away their booty, duly paid for of course. Meanwhile, restaurants, fast food outlets, office cafeterias, school canteens, coffee shops and food vendors wait for the hungry hordes to descend on them and devour the daily smorgasbord of hamburgers, pizza, Filipino food and Chinese food, and the vast array of international cuisine. The day wears on and the hour of daily deliverance comes as a blessing. From sunset onwards, the numberless, disorderly battalions of workers are washed away in the rush hour traffic, a protracted tidal wave of vehicles that could take hours to subside.

Away from the busy thoroughfares and business districts, the city is a collection of old neighborhoods with beautiful tree-lined streets, small family-run shops and stores, run-down rowhouses, and, here and there, a middle class house with a perfect garden. With a proprietary air, the residents stroll about or sit on rickety benches, amiably chatting with one another. Ambulant vendors peddle their varied merchandise—food, washtubs, house furnishings—and children play in every open space, including the street.

Even here there is work being done. A group of young men cheerfully repair the roof of an old house. A mechanic and his assistant inspect the sputtering engine of a jeepney. A tailor puts the finishing touches on a pair of pants while conversing with a friend. Three young women who operate the neighborhood beauty parlor welcome a new customer. And housewives are busy preparing the next meal.

Work for the Filipino is not just getting something done but getting it done together with others. The social aspect of work gives

ALBERTO "BULLIT" MARQUEZ

it a special significance. At planting and harvest time the farmer can always depend on his neighbors. They help him plant the seedlings in his rice paddies, then they help him harvest his crop and he in turn helps them in their fields. Fishermen band together to pull in a neighbor's boat heavily loaded with the day's catch, or they haul in a giant net from the sea, tying themselves together to pull it in with dance-like movements. Neighbors form a crew to help a villager repair the thatched roof of his house, saving his home before the heavy rains come to soak all.

Traveling through the countryside, one may be surprised to see a team of brawny, sweating men carrying an entire house on their shoulders. When a family transfers residence, they don't just leave their house and occupy another—they take their house with them and their neighbors help them carry it to its new location. The image of Filipinos carrying a house has become a symbol. The Tagalog word for cooperative effort is *bayanihan*. It is a word that is rich in meaning, for *bayan* means community, town, or nation, and *bayani* means hero. For the Filipino, work is a time for important social interaction, for strengthening friendship and building community. For the Filipino, work is also seen as a loud call to heroic dedication.

Work is the task of building the future. Parents will toil and save and sacrifice to make sure their children receive a good education. One hears stories of farmers in the highlands and lowlands who send their sons and daughters to universities in the big city. They continue to work as farmers, while their children live in the city and work as engineers, accountants, doctors, bankers, teachers, or nurses. Carpenters, laborers and taxicab drivers proudly tell of their children who have graduated with honors from distinguished colleges in the Philippines and the United States. An old lady, who makes sweets to sell in the market, glowingly speaks of her son who has just become a junior attorney in a law firm in Manila.

As people work to build their lives, a new world restlessly takes shape. There is no end to building in the city and there is no end to the urban empire spreading relentlessly to the countryside. Factories are constantly rising up as gigantic columns, beams and trusses are put together rapidly like a child's toy. Housing developments voraciously gobble up what was a bucolic realm where stalks of grain swayed gracefully in the wind. Formidable multi-storey reinforced concrete buildings are rapidly torn down to be replaced by taller, larger, glossier skyscrapers of more advanced design. One sees the next century arriving as a new city quickly rises from the ground or gradually supplants the old.

What is the symbol of the age? Is it the glitzy, hi-tech, intelligent building or the jet plane moving people towards new horizons, impatient in their wish for greater speed? Or is it the unsung worker, full of hope and longing for a better life? **R.D.P.**

A busy day in the life of President Fidel V. Ramos takes him up in the executive chopper; through the autograph-seeking crowds in the provinces; and onto the golf course—after a kiss goodbye to First Lady Amelita 'Ming' Ramos. President Ramos is credited with the economic advancement of the country and the slogan 'Philippines 2000'—which refers to the goal of achieving Newly Industrialized Country status by the year 2000.

*V*olunteer firefighters of the Chinese community douse some 200 Manila fires a year. The Association of Fire Chiefs and Fire Fighters of the Philippines, Inc. coordinate 34 local brigades, 50 firefighting engines, and over 800 volunteers to help fight fire throughout the archipelago.

The night lights of Metro Manila. Somewhere along the circumferential highway called EDSA—Epifanio de los Santos Avenue—the traffic is gridlocked during the evening rush hour. Headlights stand out as pinpoints of static light despite the fact that this photograph was taken with a long exposure.

These tricycle drivers are waiting for evening custom as people get ready to leave work and head home. Whole families can be seen jammed into these motorbike sidecars and they add to the horse-drawn carriages, jeepneys, trucks, cars and buses that cram the streets of the cities of the Philippines.

Hand-painted billboards advertising Filipino action movies look down on the exciting chaos of Manila traffic and street vendors. The Philippine film industry has been growing steadily since the 1970's and is now flourishing by popular demand. Movie theaters are open from 9a.m. to 11p.m. and films are shown continuously so the dedicated film-goer can sit and watch the same film all day if he or she so desires.

Jeepneys, 16-seater mini-vans, are the colorful public transport of the cities. Originally American army jeeps left behind by the GIs as post-war transport, the workhorse jeeps were later adapted to Filipino needs and temperaments. Taking on a decorative folk baroque style (complete with mirrors, plastic tassels and nickel stallions on the hood), jeepneys are the ubiquitous kings of the roads.

Jeepney art has evolved from folksy hand-painted panels of rural scenery to these more modern cut-and-stick plastic dolls. The saucy bikinied figures of bathing beauties at the Sarao jeepney factory in Paranaque, Manila will soon be cut out and arrayed all over the mass transport vehicles—a true reflection of the Filipino folk psyche.

A view of modern Makati from the air embodies the
pioneering spirit behind its development—from a bare
landscape to a dynamic city. In less than 50 years, the
visionary Zobel-Ayala clan has transformed a suburban
grassland into a veritable 'swankland', a paradigm for
integrated urban planning.

The Westin Philippine Plaza stands on Roxas Boulevard to
overlook Manila on three sides and the ocean on the other. On
a full occupancy day, some 800 foreign guests enjoy the breezes
off the Manila Bay and many gather by the pool at sunset to
watch the sun go down.

EDWIN TUYAY

EDWIN TUYAY

EDWIN TUYAY

CATHERINE KARNOW

Central Bank's big money-making facility, the Mint on East Avenue in Quezon City, provides the hard currency of the country. From smelting and molding the gold bars (top) to stacking the peso currency right off the press (center), to checking and classifying the shiny new coins (bottom)—it's a high value occupation, burning old and manufacturing new money.

View from the top. The Stock Exchange is wired to the Makati trading floor on Ayala Avenue; as well as to one in Ortigas. The Exchange is one of the most buoyant markets in the Asian region. From trading PhP 77 billion in 1992, the Exchange now trades five times that volume. One hundred and eighty-seven companies are now member-brokers of the local exchange.

CATHERINE KARNOW

PAUL CHESLEY

*D*on Jaime Zobel de Ayala is flanked by his sons, Jaime Augusto (left) and Fernando (right). In the Philippines, the name Ayala is synonymous with business success. The family, now in its seventh generation, manages Ayala Corporation, one of the largest and oldest conglomerates in the islands.

*T*he Philippine Stock Exchange Building on Ayala Avenue in Makati is perhaps the country's best symbol of financial and commercial progress. This impressive building, designed by National Artist for Architecture Leandro Locsin, stands in the heart of Makati, the swamp town which was transformed into swank city and is one of the most expensive pieces of real estate in the Philippines today.

The morning flood of workers cross the bridge from Olongapo into the New Subic Bay Freeport. Subic, a former U.S. Navy base has continued to prosper economically (right) despite the fact that the navy personnel have now left. The Glorietta Mall in Makati (opposite) does a roaring trade every day of the week.

The Philippine flag flutters over Manila's historic Corregidor Island—and is carried all over the world on the side of the country's national airline (right). Corregidor was captured from the United States by the Japanese during World War II.

*P*hilippine Airlines (PAL), the nation's oldest carrier service, runs a tight ship. Hundreds of maintenance personnel take pride in keeping the extensive PAL fleet airworthy and spiffy clean.

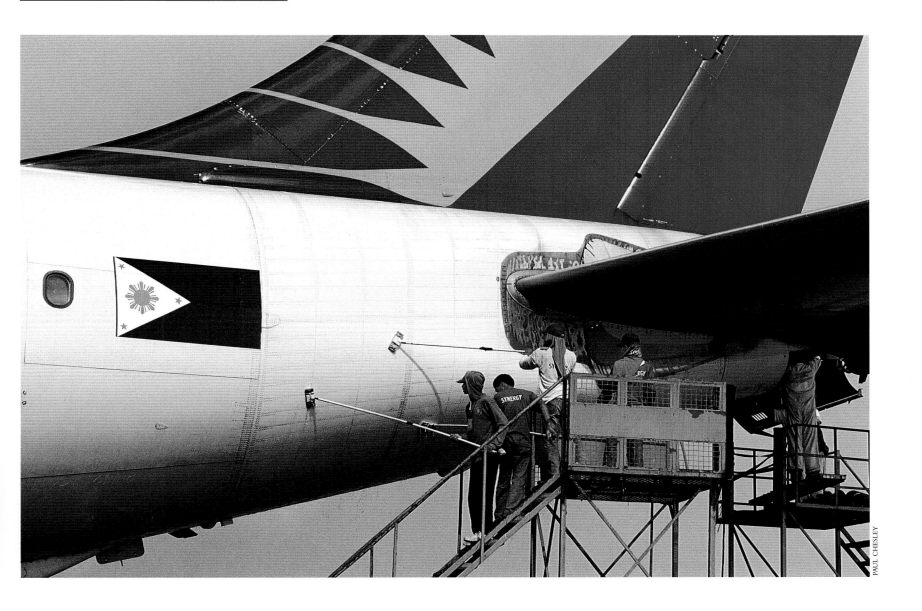

Down on the ground, PAL's maintenance complex works 24-hours-a-day to ensure a reliable flight schedule. PAL personnel toil in clockwork precision, maintaining aircraft engines (above); providing inflight meals (top right); checking cabin interior amenities (center right); or supplying ground support (bottom right). These people are all geared to one goal: safe, reliable and convenient flights.

*D*oris Magsaysay Ho, Chief Executive Officer of Magsaysay Shipping Lines, Inc., runs businesses connected with ships and tourism. As the President of the Touristbelt Businessmen's Association, Ms. Ho is an inspired advocate of the restoration and preservation of old Manila landmarks. She's also a tireless fund-raiser and volunteer for many charities and civic causes, when she's not running a shipping company.

*M*anila's port area on the bay outside Intramuros is the bustling pier zone where mountains of plump white sacks of sugar arrive from the Visayas destined for domestic and international distribution. With agriculture as the basis of economic life, sugarcane, coconut, abaca, tobacco and pineapples are grown for worldwide export.

People work to make things better. In Manila, a dock worker takes the scaffolding one step higher (right). In Ormoc, Leyte (above), massive steel girders are pulled into place to construct a new gymnasium. After 1991's tragedy of flash floods (caused by over-logging) which washed away parts of Ormoc, the town revives by building a large gym for sports as well as for evacuation and shelter—just in case.

GUIDO ALBERTO ROSSI

A bird's eye view of the roadway through the Rice Bowl of Luzon. The North Expressway starts at the outer edge of Metro Manila and crosses northward to the mountains, traversing the central plains of Bulacan, Pampanga and Tarlac. It passes over the 87,000 hectares of devastation left by the lahar (mudslide caused by volcanic ash) that accompanied Mount Pinatubo's eruption in June 1991.

PRESCIANO (SONNY) YABAO

*S*tar Motors is a large vehicle-assembly plant located in an industrial park in Sta. Rosa, Laguna—one of the towns within easy reach of Manila experiencing new industrial development. Nissan gives jobs to skilled workers from the Southern Tagalog area. The assembly factory turns out a wide variety of vehicles, from Safari Patrols, to Eagle four wheel drive pick-ups and Nissan Terranos.

A straight, steely line runs from the Ilocos region to America, land of the immigrant—along the finest road network in the archipelago. This sturdy iron bridge on the long highway between north and south Ilocos, carries Ilocano immigrants directly to planes winging to the Western world.
DOMINIC SANSONI

Following pages:
A Mangyan tribesman stuck in the mud in Mindoro. His mouth is reddened by chewing betelnut, a leaf from a narcotic plant. The sturdy jeep and its hapless passengers were stuck midstream for over two hours.
ALBERTO 'BULLIT' MARQUEZ

A yoke of green bananas hitches a ride to market on the carabao, the Philippine beast of burden. Carabao of Samar are kept busy by the demands of rice-culture; turning the soil to prepare for planting requires long hours of work with the carabao pulling the plow through the soil. Afterwards, the great horned beast happily cools off in the mud.

A Hanunoo Mangyan mother migrates with the family possessions balanced on her back—carried in a big head-strap basket. The whole family moved across Mindoro Island tugging their pigs beside them; until lowlanders bought their animals along the way. The family, who practice a slash-and-burn form of agriculture, look to settle anew and build a kainging, *a vegetable patch on the mountainside.*

ALBERTO 'BULLIT' MARQUEZ

Rice farmers start very young these days. The baby in diapers gets into the wet mud of a rice paddy in Lao-Ang, northern Samar. Following after the carabao and the heavy plow, the whole family gets down into the paddy to break and turn the mud, in preparation for the easy hand-planting of rice-seedlings the next morning.

To market, to market, go the four black pigs of Siquijor. Once a week the livestock market of Malapatay on Siquijor Island, off Negros, sees these squealing animals being bought to be raised in other towns and neighboring islands. Siquijor is known as a spooky island, which you travel to by boat and come back from on a broomstick, with a squeal.

A whole calf a-roasting over open coals is a common sight in the marketplace. In Divisoria, the wholesalers' market in old Manila, animals turn for hours over the coals, until finally they are purchased as the centerpieces of fiesta tables. The roast pig or Lechon *(right)*, is the Filipino fiesta favorite and is served with a sweet liver sauce.

The golden lechon line-up: crispy roast suckling pigs stand ready-made for a fiesta with the whole village. This icon of Filipino hospitality (if not cuisine) at its finest is found all around Manila, especially at Lydia's Lechon on the southern end of Roxas Boulevard in Baclaran; or at the original Mang Tomas in La Loma on the north end of town.

PAUL CHESLEY

GUEORGUI PINKHASSOV

*T*hree o'clock in the morning signals the most bustling of all market scenes. Fishermen haul their massive buckets of fresh fish to the wholesale wet market of Navotas, Rizal. The busy scene above contrasts with this crustacean trading post in Maguindanao, right. The Filipino menu includes blue crabs, black crabs, brown crabs, alimasag and alimango, talangka, the smallest, tastiest one, and coconut crab, the largest crustacean which indeed climbs coconut trees to reach the fruit.

MICHAEL FREEMAN

LEONG KA TAI

MICHAEL S. YAMASHITA

*B*uying fish in every town, the Philippines. Fresh galunggong *(above)*, the finger-sized ocean fish that feeds the masses, is the basic measure of the relative cost of food in the country. Dried fish and squid on the bilao, the round woven tray *(left)*, look good and cook better. Drying fish is the most popular method of preserving fish in the Philippines. Small seafood is split at the back and laid flat in two halves. After a good rub in salt or a soak in brine, the fish are laid out to dry.

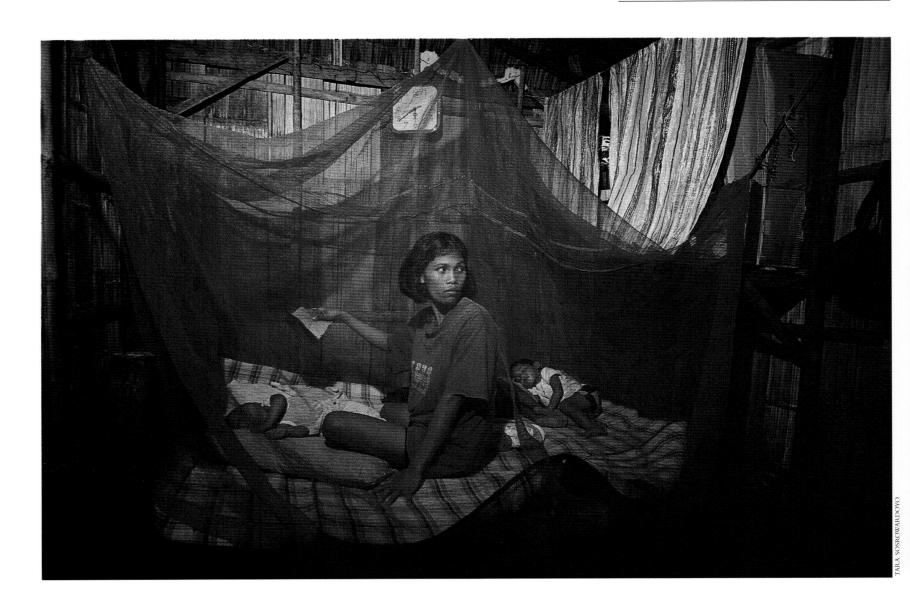

TARA SOSROWARDOYO

*T*his Mangyan tribesman eats kamote, the sweet potato farmed in the hinterlands of Mindoro Island, south of Luzon. While Mangyans are simple folk who have migrated to the uplands by choice, they remain prey to lowlanders' exploitation. Culturally they possess a unique tradition in poetry and music and write in a syllabic Indic script which they etch on bamboo.

ALBERTO 'BULLIT' MARQUEZ

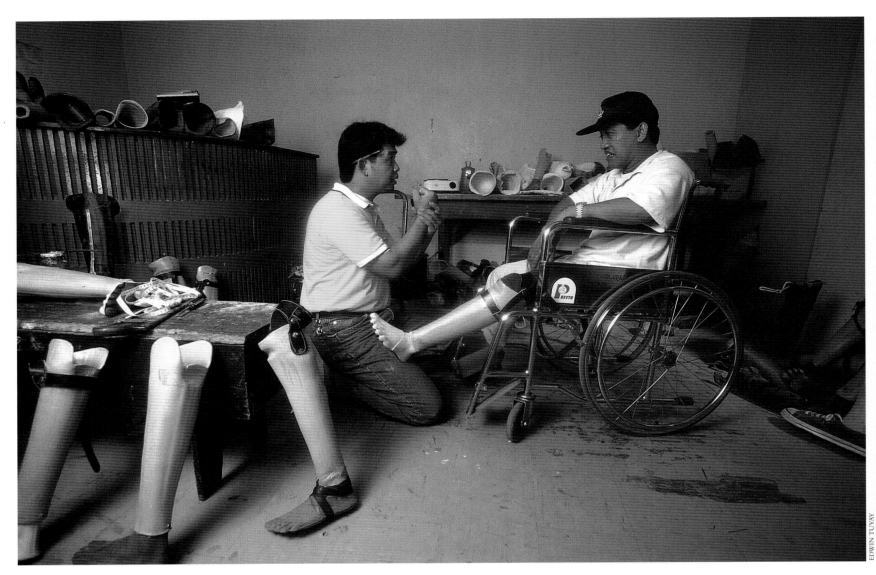

*B*race-maker Rufino Regino, a disabled employee of the
National Orthopedic Hospital, fits a prosthetic leg onto patient
Dominador Colibao, a worker who lost both legs to
electrocution (above). *T*he lady in the rocking chair (right) is
the 96-year-old Lola Valentine, Mercedes de Leon. Born in
June 1900, in Pangasinan, she is this year's Miss Valentine in
the Golden Acres retirement home. An old-fashioned Mum
lovingly grooms her son of white hair (opposite).

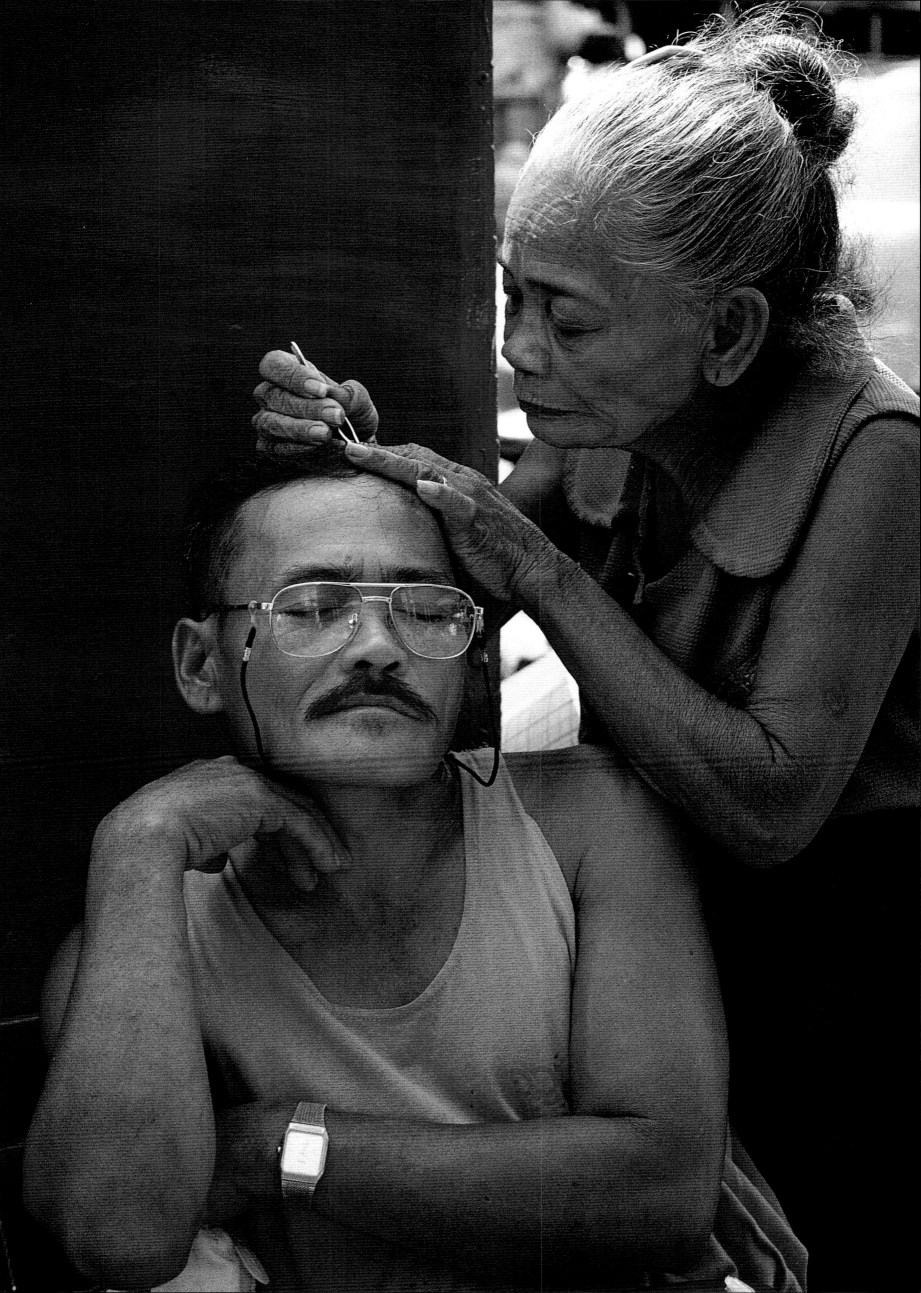

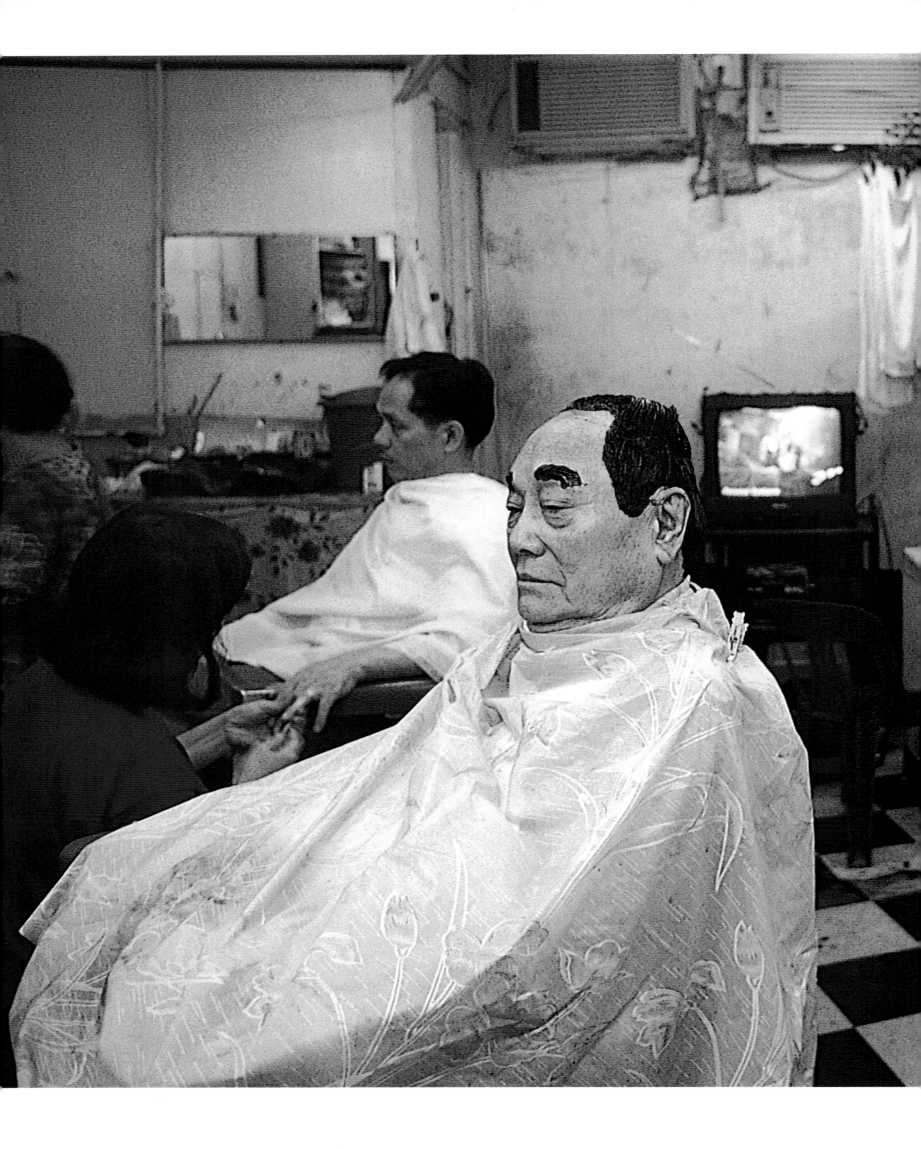

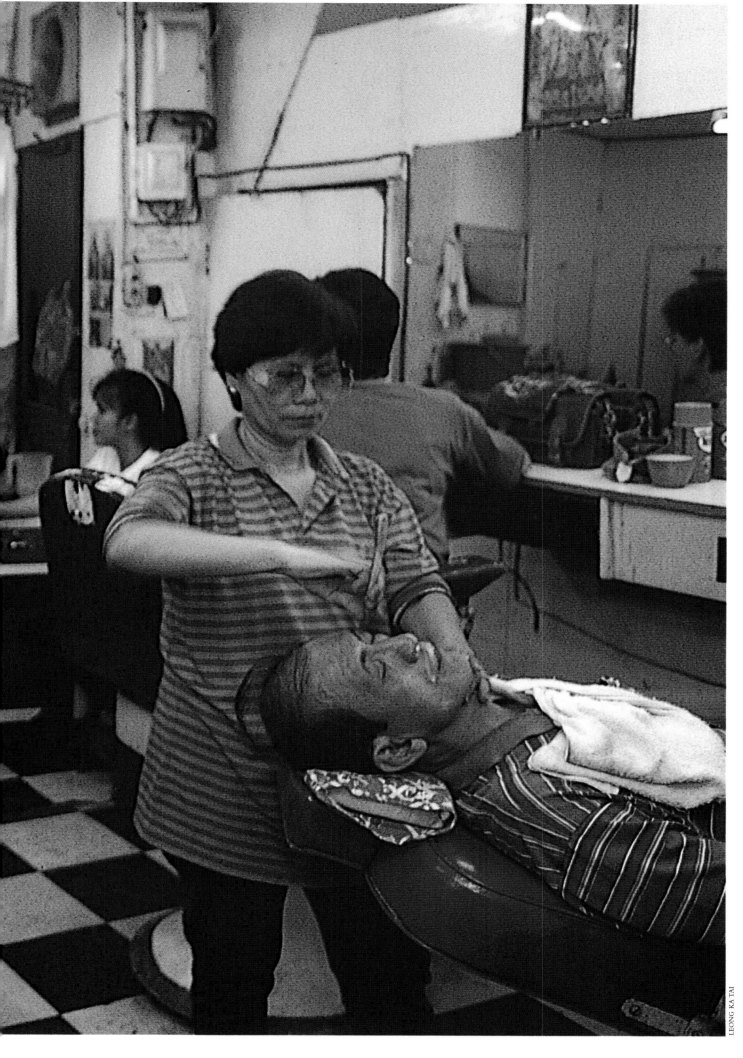

An old-fashioned haircut in an old-fashioned barbershop in Binondo, Manila's Chinatown, is a throwback to another time. The barbershop in the back alley is the traditional place to hear neighborhood news and gossip. Mga kuwentong barbero *(barbershop stories)* is a Tagalog phrase which refers to the exaggerated tales heard from under a hot face towel.

Beauty parlor culture. Ness Astilla, stylist in a Mona Lisa tie, does make-up on Marivic Garcia, 18, hair model at the Ricky Reyes Hair Salon. The irrepressible Ricky Reyes is a success story of the '90s—he has established a dozen chic hair salons around Manila and a big school for hairdressers.

MARY ELLEN MARK

A costumed couple enjoy a Sparklers' party (above). The Sparklers are a society of elder matrons and widows who are ballroom-dancing their years away with professional dance instructors (now called 'Attorneys.') The ladies rendezvous at the Manila Polo Club to dance graceful tangos, rumbas and pasa dobles—with an aplomb that belies their (average 68) years.

MARY ELLEN MARK

Imelda Cojuangco is a dazzling lady; widow-matriarch of a powerful clan; the patroness of religious and arts projects (she received a Papal Award for her support of the Church's activities); and in society, a most sought-after godmother at baptisms and guest at weddings and gala affairs. Imelda follows her own sense of style: pure haute-couture, ultra-feminine.

An orphaned baby is coddled at the Asilo de Molo in Iloilo, where 15 toddlers share the common nursery. Founded in 1912 by Bishop Dennis Dougherty and managed by the kindly Sisters of the Daughters of Charity of Saint Vincent de Paul, the Asilo has grown famous for the fine hand embroidery turned out by orphaned girls under 16.

The giddy girls of the Asilo de Molo are showered with affection at an early age. The Asilo is known for fostering virtuous young women who practice respect for human dignity, compassion and responsibility. Girls over 16 are allowed to stay at the home until they can find work. Missy (bottom right) sings on the karaoke, unaware of her small audience.

JOSE ENRIQUE SORIANO

This bantam weightlifter carries the weight of big dreams in a small-time gymnasium in Dumaguete, Negros Oriental. Dumaguete is well known for Silliman University—the only Protestant university in the Philippines, the anthropological museum, excellent diving sites and delicious seafood.

EDWIN TUVAY

ROBIN MOYER

GUEORGUI PINKHASSOV

PAUL CHESLEY

Classical music reaches all ends of the archipelago. Juanito Napay, a 98-year-old maestro teaches three Korean girls to play the violin in the shadow of Mount Mayon in Legaspi, Albay (top). Young ballerinas of the Quezon City Performing Arts Studio pose shyly after their community recital at the Quezon City Auditorium (above). The Performing Arts Studio is a program sponsored by the City Mayor, Ismael Mathay Jr., exclusively for the urban poor of Quezon City.

A 'Baby Ballet' class at Tita Vella's School of Ballet is something that every well-turned out little girl does on Saturday mornings—to grow up as a graceful Filipino woman. Classical ballet came to the Philippines in the '50s, and after five decades of dancing, the country has produced superb ballerinas for the world, such as Maniya Barredo and Anna Villadolid.

*M*r. Asia, Sammy Ayochoc, all pectorals and biceps, lifts
Ackhaya Casey, a tiny babe in Baguio City. Pumping iron
and lifting weights to sculpt a beautiful body is a favorite art
among provincial males. Here Sammy carries his best trophy,
his new daughter.

Mother and child with a new flowered hat. From the time Filipinos are born, they are handled with abundant affection by family and friends. They are constantly surrounded by people and are always part of social gatherings—where they learn to sing and dance for their elders.

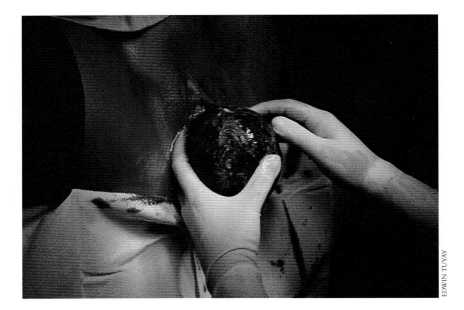

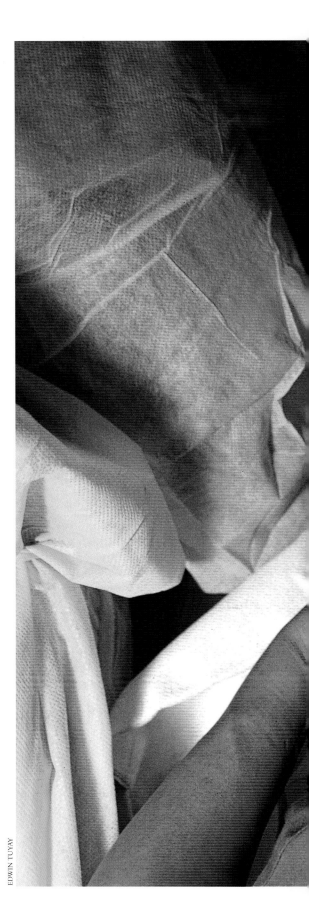

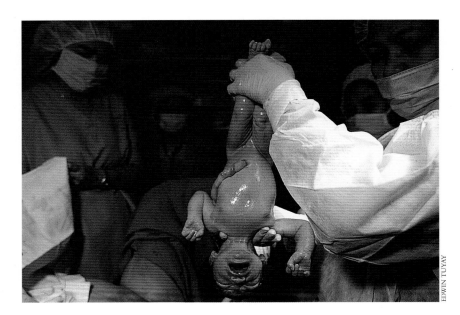

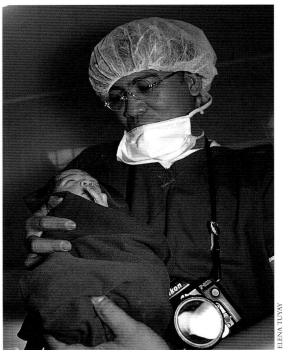

*O*ur Shoot Week baby, born on October 11th, 1995, to news photographer Edwin Tuyay, was aptly named Nirvana. Tuyay's wife Maria Elena, also a photographer, delivered a healthy 6.9 lb baby girl at the Dr. Jesus Delgado Memorial Hospital in Quezon City. When the proud papa held his new daughter for the first time, Elena grabbed the camera and took the photographer's picture for posterity (left, bottom).

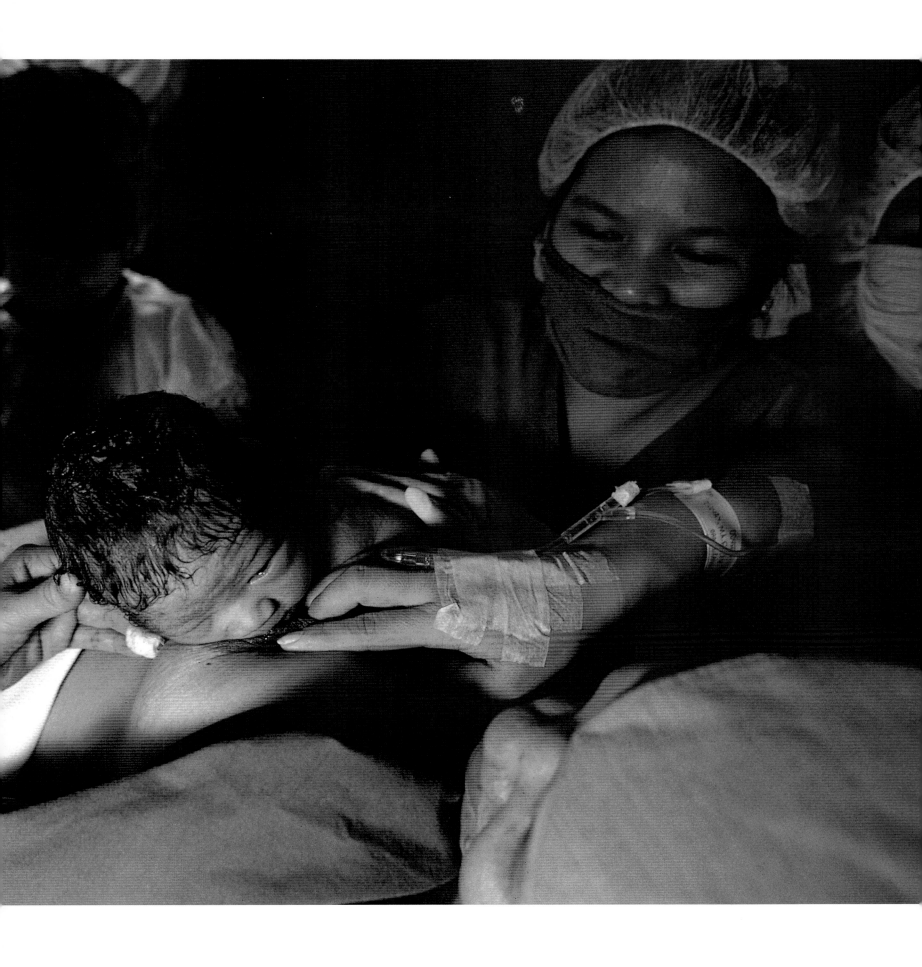

The gentle smile of a child of Tondo, Manila. His joy at being carried over a parental shoulder belies his depressed surroundings near the pier area of the metropolis. Population density runs high among urban poor families in their ramshackle huts in Tondo—the stifling result of mass migration into the big city from the provinces.

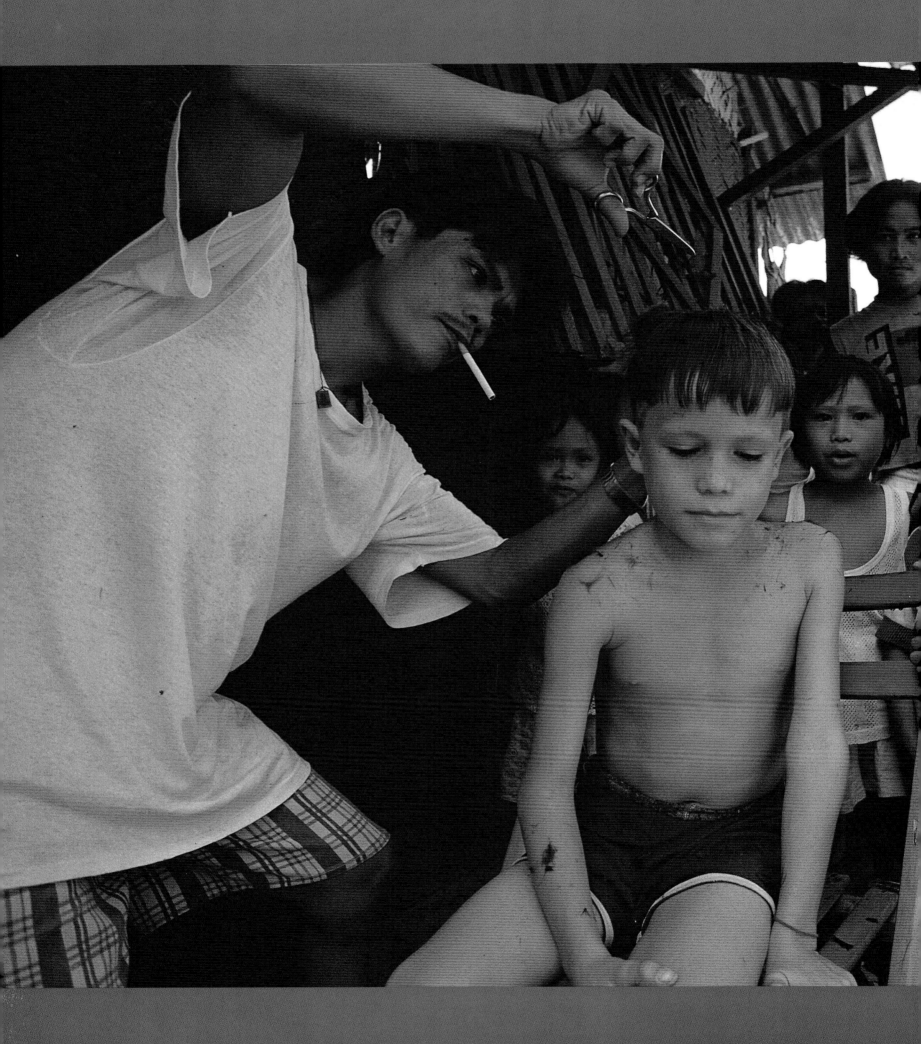

A young Australian-Asian from Clark Field, Pampanga, eight-year-old John Anos was born to Rosemarie, a former bar worker, and an Australian now living in Melbourne. John has grown up with his Filipino family and friends and is in the second grade at school.

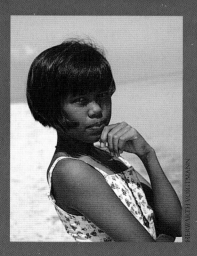

An endearing tot with a strong Chinese heritage (opposite).
Almost 70% of Filipinos are under 25 years old. Life for
them is laughter and love, school and play, in shopping malls,
with dad's fishing nets, and out on the river.

*I*n the Zamboanga Hermosa parade (above), a contingent of college students perform syncopated steps to the music. Doll-like masked performers ready for the Bacolod Masskara parade (right), practice their paces in front of the Negros Oriental provincial capital building.

HIROJI KUBOTA

KAREN KASMAUSKI

HIROJI KUBOTA

ROBIN MOYER

A group of Igorot tribal dancers (above) in the Zamboanga Hermosa parade celebrate the Virgin Mary, the mother figure of Roman Catholics. The kiddie parade in Sorsogon in Bicol (left) sends the youngsters off early in the morning with drums, tambourines and batons.

*F*ollowing pages: The smiling Sister rides a Mickey Mouse tricycle across town. While the Philippines is a Roman Catholic enclave in Asia, the religious practice of the Church has so blended with the native folk practice of the tribes that a large religious community is needed to maintain the faith.
DOMINIC SANSONI

MICHAEL FREEMAN

HIROJI KUBOTA

A Mangyan matron dons her finery to descend to the market in the lowlands (opposite). The Manobo tribe of north Cotabato holds stallion fights down in Makilala, Kidapawan, on the occasion of the Pama'as or Thanksgiving Festival. The winner of two rounds of stallion fights is Tora-Tora, a famous fighting horse of the region (above). Another fighting sport is cockfighting (sabong). Roosters are pampered game birds— massaged and exercised from dawn to dusk in preparation for the Sunday match (left).

EDWIN TUYAY

EDWIN TUYAY

A light-hearted moment at the Golden Acres old folks home in Bagobantay, Pag-Asa, Quezon City (above); Lola Pacita Garcia, 75, senior citizen with her walker, laughs with Lolo Francisco Paragas, 73, her junior. The senior citizens' band (right) strikes up a happy tune to entertain their fellow elders. Senior citizens are admitted at 60, but most of the residents are aged between 65 and 70.

Manila's outré couturiers have a creative stage in many hotels, where fashion shows come with the lunch (opposite). Beauty contests are also a Filipino favorite (above), with hours of preparation (below left) and hope going into the beauty "Dream Machine."

*M*elanie Marquez, model par excellence. She was just a lanky 13-year-old when she was discovered for the fashion ramp in 1977. From there, Melanie went from rags to riches, fame and world titles: She was Miss International in 1979 and a 'Supermodel' in New York in 1984.

*T*he 'Prince of Fashion' creates another fillip to fashion. In the salon of the hottest young fashion couturier in Manila today, Inno Sotto examines one of his latest creations, based on the tribal tattoos of the Ifugao tribe. Filipinos love their fashion shows as they bring fantasy to life on the ramp.

KAREN KASMAUSKI

*B*eauties blooming in the mirrors. Contestants touch up their make-up during rehearsals for the beauty pageant of the Bacolod Masskara Festival. People of the Visayas are usually described as being slower in their pace and talk with a lilt in their speech. Winning a local beauty pageant can mean going on to become prominent politically.

*L*ooking for Miss Manila 1995 at the Westin Philippine Plaza Hotel. The air vibrates with the glamour and glitz of a beauty contest. Filipinos take their beauty queens seriously and are proud of the beautiful women who have won international titles over the decades, such as Gloria Diaz, Gemma Cruz, Aurora Pijuan, Margie Moran and Melanie Marquez.

ROMEO GACAD

CATHERINE KARNOW

A night out at Zu, the trendy disco-lounge at the Shangri-La, Makati, Manila (opposite). Stylish dancers take the spotlight in Tacloban City, Leyte (above). The young couple perform the sweeping dips and turns of a dazzling exhibition dance with bravado before the oldies ballroom group takes over the local night club. A couple dance the night away at the Blue Café in Malate, Manila (left).

All that liner and lipstick: It's the show-biz make-up session backstage before the Blue Café impersonations show. The popular gay nightclub in the bohemian Remedios Circle neighborhood pulls in the crowds with its glittery Friday night productions. On other days of the week, the dancers and entertainers return to their professional roles as designers, actors, artists and couturiers.

CATHERINE KARNOW

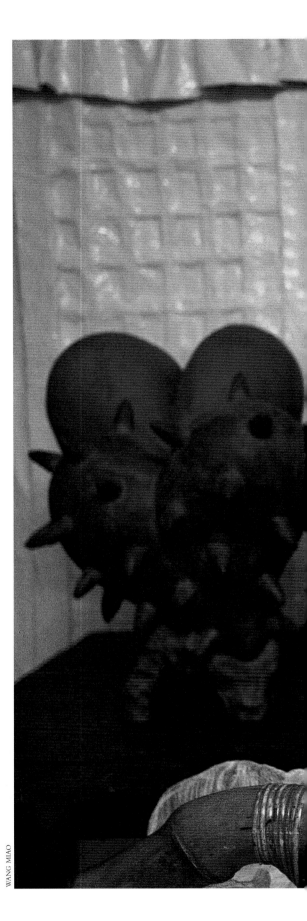

WANG MIAO

WANG MIAO

The painter Lao Lianben leads the field in Philippine abstract art. Lao executes his work on vast canvases where he works the surface of the painting into many complex textures. Lao restricts his palette to bare tones of grey, ivory and black. The artist's works have been both criticised and praised as "objects of meditation."

Julie Lluch, feminist artist and sculptress, creates life-sized terracotta figures to keep her outré company—and to work out her own tensions with the structures of Philippine society. Lluch's terracotta busts, acrylic-painted in her sensitive social-realistic style, are singular works coveted by her subjects (personal friends) and their onlookers. Her self-portrait demonstrates her feelings about housework.

Following pages: Artists of all types (left to right) flourish around the country: Bencab, painter; Mariel Francisco, Gilda Fernando, Fe Maria Arriola, creative editors; Nonon Padilla, theater director cum laude: Barge Ramos and two models, couturier and his angels: Imelda Cajipe-Endaya, visual artist, installationist: Virginia Moreno, poetess, and her brother Pitoy, couturier: Arturo Luz, National Artist; film director

Celso Ad Castillo; Joey Ayala, folk singer; Grace Nono and the Pinikpikan band: Ramon Orlina, sculptor in glass; Impy Pilapil, sculptress in glass; Surrealist artist Onib Olmedo; Bong Revilla, actor and Cavite Vice Governor; "Frankie" Sionil José, novelist, PEN-mogul; Odette Alcantara, art patroness, gallery owner and writer.

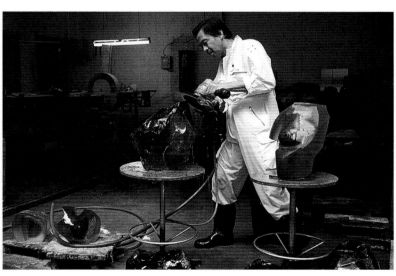

*Bacolod's Masskara Festival began in 1980 when the
Negrenses put on brave faces (smiling masks) amidst the fall in
the price of sugar. Week-long celebrations climax with a street
parade in fantasy costumes and smiling masks.*

FIESTA
ISLANDS

Evangelization laid the groundwork for the establishment of what became a Filipino nation. To convert a dispersed pagan population to Christianity, it was first necessary to bring the scattered populace "under the (church) bells." That meant living in communities. The word comes from the Latin, *communis*, which means camaraderie. The Spanish soon discovered that, in the Philippines, the common values of the community were most obviously expressed in the form of the town fiesta.

All communities celebrate their fiesta and all the major church festivities, **Holy Week**, **Christmas** and **All Saints' Day**. The church calendar is luni-solar. So we have movable and immovable feasts. **Christmas, All Saints' Day** and the feasts of individual saints always fall on fixed days in the Gregorian calendar. But movable feasts are determined by their relationship to **Easter** (which is always commemorated on the Sunday following the first moon after the vernal equinox).

Every town has its fiesta. This celebration is held on the feast of the town's patron saint and that day marks the anniversary of the town's founding. Two different towns may celebrate the feasts of the same saint, but the fiesta can be totally different. Classic examples are the fiestas of *Pulilan* and *Lucban* in *Luzon*. Both towns pay homage to a common patron saint, San Isidro Labrador, but in *Pulilan*, a carabao festival takes place; in *Lucban*, the **pahiyas** takes place—every home is decorated with a unique folk art—rice paste that has been shaped into the form of a leaves and tinted in all colors.

All Saints' Day is celebrated on November 1st in *every cemetery* in the Philippines. The graves are cleaned and decorated and people literally spend the whole day and night with their departed relatives and friends who they believe are now in heaven.

In *Kalibo, Aklan, Visayas*, the feast of the **Santo Niño**, or Holy Child, has eclipsed even the feast of their own town fiesta. *Kalibo* was founded in 1581 and got its name from *sang Ka libo*, one thousand, because that was said to be the number of natives baptized in one day by a missionary during the **Feast of Saint John the Baptist. The Feast of the Baptist** is generally celebrated with the splashing of water. But in *Kalibo*, the splashing of water on **Saint John's Day** takes a back seat to the **Ati-Atihan**, the noisy and colorful fiesta which is the Philippines' greatest tourist attraction.

The **Moriones of Marinduque** ranks next in popularity with tourists. This fiesta takes place during **Passion Week**. The feast culminates during **Easter** on the **Sunday of the Resurrection of our Lord**. It is 'the solemnity of solemnities', as the event of Resurrection is the foundation of the faith.

The year ends with the biggest fiesta of them all—**Christmas. Christmas** used to be a 21-day celebration ending with **Epiphany** (on January 6th). But the **Epiphany** is now celebrated on the Sunday between January 2nd and 5th so **Christmas** can last up to 23 days—surely the longest celebration of this fiesta anywhere in the world?

PASSION WEEK

Passion Week is one of the most intense weeks of fiesta in the Philippines and all of these photographs show it being celebrated in various forms. The Moriones of Marinduque (immediate right) is just one example of the many highly individual celebrations that take place during this time. The Moriones reenacts the legend of the partially blind soldier, Longinus, who pierced Christ's side with his spear. When Longinus speared Christ's side, the Lord's blood spurted on his sightless eye and its vision was restored. When Longinus tells of Christ's divinity his soldiers turn against him and kill him.

THE ATI-ATIHAN

The most fun-filled Philippine fiesta is the Ati-Atihan of Kalibo which takes place every third weekend in January. It is a tribute to the cannoneers of Fort Santo Niño who repulsed a huge Muslim raid. Gunpowder smoke sooted the faces of the artillerists, so they emerged from battle looking like dark-skinned Atis (the original natives of Kalibo). Looking like Atis became the motif of the celebration. The revelers repeat the gunner's battle cry, *Hala Bira! Hit 'em!* followed by the victorious shout *Viva Santo Niño!* Today, the Ati-Atihan is an audience participation spectacle powered by the fantasies of every participant.

THE HOLY CROSS OF MAY

Officially abolished by Pope XXIII in 1960, the Invention of the Cross is a feast held on May 3rd to commemorate Dowager-Queen Helena's finding of the true cross of Christ in Calvary. In the Philippines, this festival is celebrated throughout the month of May with a beauty pageant in the guise of a religious procession. The most beautiful girls in the district portray the 75-year-old Queen Helena and selected female characters from the Bible. It is the Philippine equivalent of the Queen of the May. The Vatican abolition has had no effect on the popularity of the festival.

THE PATRON SAINT OF FARMERS

The feast of San Isidro "the Plowman" commemorates the Philippine entry into the agricultural era. This happened when Spanish missionaries introduced the plow and the Asian water buffalo to the islands. They were respectively presented as the instrument and animal of San Isidro. No invention has exceeded the plow in lightening man's task. The shift from hoe to plow upgraded Filipinos' status from subsistence to surplus farmers. Providentially, San Isidro's feast (May 15th) coincides perfectly with the start of the rice-planting season. His festival is a homage to the carabao and an offering for a beautiful harvest.

CHRISTMAS

Christmas could not fall at a better time in the Philippines—right in the middle of the rice harvesting season. When people have the means to celebrate. Christmas officially starts on December 16th with Novena Mass and nationwide lantern festivals (right). The Mass is celebrated at an ungodly hour—four o'clock in the morning! This is to accommodate the farmers who hear Mass, before rushing to their harvest. On Christmas Eve, a man and a woman reenact Saint Joseph's and the Virgin Mary's quest for an inn. After being refused lodgings in several homes, the couple end up in church in time for the Midnight Mass.

JANUARY

◆**SANTO NIÑO PROCESSION** Manila, last Sunday: Winding its long way down Roxas Boulevard towards the Quirino Grandstand, this procession—participated in by thousands of devotees—sees 300 images of the Christ child borne in carriages bedecked with flowers and lights. ◆ **SINULOG** Cebu City, third weekend: A homage to the historic Santo Niño marked with a solemn Mass and a parade through the streets of people in papier mâché figures and wildly bright costumes waving their arms in a special dance through the *sulog* (flow of water).

FEBRUARY

◆**HARI-RAYA POASA** Zamboanga, Sulu, Lanao, Cotabato, Palawan, a movable feast: Celebrated after the 29th day of the Ramadan fast, Hari-Raya Poasa is a fast-breaking holiday. The Imam awaits everyone at the mosque for an hour of prayer, followed by a ceremony where friends and relatives ask for forgiveness for past offenses. After this, people join in horse racing and carabao-fighting while others watch colorful boat races. In the evening the family assembles for a special dinner feast. ◆**CHINESE NEW YEAR** nationwide, late January or early February, depending on the lunar calendar: The Chinese community celebrates its New Year by watching energetic lion dances, elaborate firework displays and Chinese opera performances—while they feast on delicacies.

MARCH

◆**LAMI-LAMIHAN** Lamitan, Basilan, 23rd-24th: A festival which celebrates the unique cultural heritage of the Yakans of Basilan. Native braves perform the famous Yakan war dance (called the *tumahik*) while beautiful local women dance to the beat of the *agong*, *kulintang* and *gandang*. ◆**ARAW NG DABAW** Davao City, 10th-16th: Cultural performances highlight this celebration of the city's Charter Day. Dancers dressed in colorful and intricately handwoven indigenous costumes entertain the crowds.

APRIL

◆**PENITENCIA** nationwide, Good Friday: Penitents flog their backs with whips or trudge through the streets carrying wooden crosses in honor of Christ's passion and death in atonement for personal sins. The day's climactic penitential rite occurs with the actual crucifixion of several penitent volunteers. ◆**LANDING OF MAGELLAN** San Nicolas City, 24th: Cebu celebrates the first Catholic Mass (on Limasawa Island) and the occasion of the first baptism on Philippine soil.

MAY

◆**OBANDO FERTILITY RITES** Obando, Bulacan, 17th-19th: This festival honors three saints: Santa Clara, patron saint of the childless; San Pascual Baylon, a model of religious virtues; and Nuestra Señora de Salambao, to whom the town's fishermen pray for a bountiful catch. Women dance in the streets to the tune of Santa Clara's melody, praying for the blessing of a child. ◆**ANTIPOLO PILGRIMAGE** Antipolo, Rizal, month-long: People walk to Antipolo to pay homage to *Nuestra Señora de la Paz y Buen Viaje*, Our Lady of Peace and Good Voyage, a three-century-old image of the Blessed Virgin.

FIESTA CALENDAR

Quiapo's folksy religious fare includes third-eye amulets and green plastic crucifixes.

JUNE

◆**PARADA NG LECHON** Balayan, Batangas, 24th: A huge parade of golden-red, crispy lechon is the highlight of the feast of San Juan in Balayan, Batangas. ◆**APALIT RIVER FESTIVAL** Apalit, Pampanga, 28th-30th: Dedicated to San Pedro and San Pablo, this three-day festival's highlight is the traditional fluvial procession along the Pampanga River of the image of San Pedro dressed in its finest robes.

JULY

◆**KINABAYO FESTIVAL** Dapitan, Zamboanga del Norte, 24th-25th: A reenactment of the battle between Santiago's troops and the Moors in a street play known as *Kinabayo*, acted out on hobbyhorses. ◆**SANTA MARTA RIVER FESTIVAL** Pateros, Metro Manila, 29th: The town, made famous by the Filipino delicacy called *balut* honors their patron saint.

AUGUST

◆**KAGAYHAAN FESTIVAL** Cagayan de Oro, 26th-28th: A homage to San Agustin, the patron saint of Cagayan de Oro, is marked with a parade of civic-military groups and costumed cultural communities. ◆**BAGUIO DAY** Baguio City, 29th August-2nd September: A commemoration of the Foundation Day of the city with an intense week-long series of diverse cultural activities.

SEPTEMBER

◆**SEÑOR SAN MIGUEL** Iligan, Lanao del Norte, 29th: In homage to the Archangel Michael, the people of Iligan don elaborate costumes to depict what folklore has said to be the saint's victory over the devil. ◆**T'BOLI TRIBAL FESTIVAL** Lake Sebu, South Cotabato, third week: A thanksgiving festival that stems from the belief of the T'bolis in a *Lem-lunay*, or golden age. This festival aims to reenergize the people to work for this state of being.

OCTOBER

◆**MASSKARA** Bacolod City, movable feast: An expression of the Negrenses' fortitude and unconquerable soul. Masskara features a mardi gras of revelers wearing papier mâché masks (see page 236) and dancing to the beat of drums and the hollering of onlookers. ◆**FEAST OF CHRIST THE KING** nationwide, 25th: An annual afternoon procession in honor of Jesus Christ.

NOVEMBER

◆**UNDAS** nationwide, 1st: Despite its solemn undertones, Undas, or All Saints' Day, is a joyous one for Filipinos. Based on the belief that the souls of one's loved ones return to their earthly home on this day, the 'reunion' is marked by abundant food, a gathering of the whole clan, and much noise. ◆**FEAST OF SAN CLEMENTE** Angono, Rizal, fourth week: Angono fishermen's thanksgiving festival in honor of, San Clemente. The image of the saint is carried on a barge to the lake and back to the church in a colorful display.

DECEMBER

◆**GIANT LANTERN FESTIVAL** San Fernando, Pampanga, 23rd-24th: The people of San Fernando show off their craft; the most colorful, and intricate *parol* (star-shaped lanterns), in a big, bright and truly festive parade. ◆**PASTORES DE BELEN** Legaspi City, month-long: Groups of brightly-costumed boys and girls called *pastores* travel from house to house dancing and singing Spanish or Bicolano songs, expressing the joy the shepherds must have felt when they heard the news of the birth of the Messiah. **A.R.R.**

21 FILIPINO THINGS

An **ARCHIPELAGO** *of 7,107 islands with a coastline twice that of the United States:* **BAMBOO** *is the islands' prime building and craft material: The* **BANAUE RICE TERRACES** *are the eighth wonder of the world for Filipinos: Every man gets married in a* **BARONG TAGALOG***, the Philippine national dress: Filipinos look at the world through* **CAPIZ** *windows, made from translucent shells: The Philippines is Southeast Asia's only* **CATHOLIC** *country:* **FAITH HEALERS** *cure without drugs or knives for those who believe.*

WANG MIAO

RIO HELMI

LUCA INVERNIZZI TETTONI

PRESCIANO (SONNY) YABAO

PAUL CHESLEY

OLIVER STREWE

CATHERINE KARNOW

There are an estimated 70 million **FILIPINOS** living all over the archipelago: The Philippines has a rich tradition of **FOLK DANCING**: Streets are jammed with **JEEPNEYS** taking and fetching people from work: **JOSE RIZAL**, physician, novelist, poet, linguist, artist, scientist and historian is the Philippine national hero: **LECHON**, roast suckling pig, is fiesta food: The Philippine Islands are famous the world over for growing the sweetest **MANGOES**: Filipinos love **MUSIC**, from traditional favorites to American country and western.

CATHERINE KARNOW

PAUL CHESLEY

RICHARD BALDOVINO

LUCA INVERNIZZI TETTONI

STEPHEN PAGE

RIO HELMI

DOMINIC SNASONI

240

PAUL CHESLEY

EMIL DAVOCOL

STEPHEN PAGE

ROBIN MOYER

LUCA INVERNIZZI TETTONI

EMIL DAVOCOL

EDWIN TUYAY

*The archipelago's favorite sport is cockfighting, known as **SABONG**: The **SAMPAGUITA** was declared the national flower in 1934: Most Filipino homes have a **SANTOS** either for the home altar or to ensure good luck: The most popular language of the islands is **TAGALOG**: The three dozen major ethnic groups of the Philippines make for a diverse patchwork of peoples all belonging to their own **TRIBES**: Philippine **VOLCANOES** belong to the Ring of Fire: The **WILDLIFE** of the Philippines is uniquely diverse.*

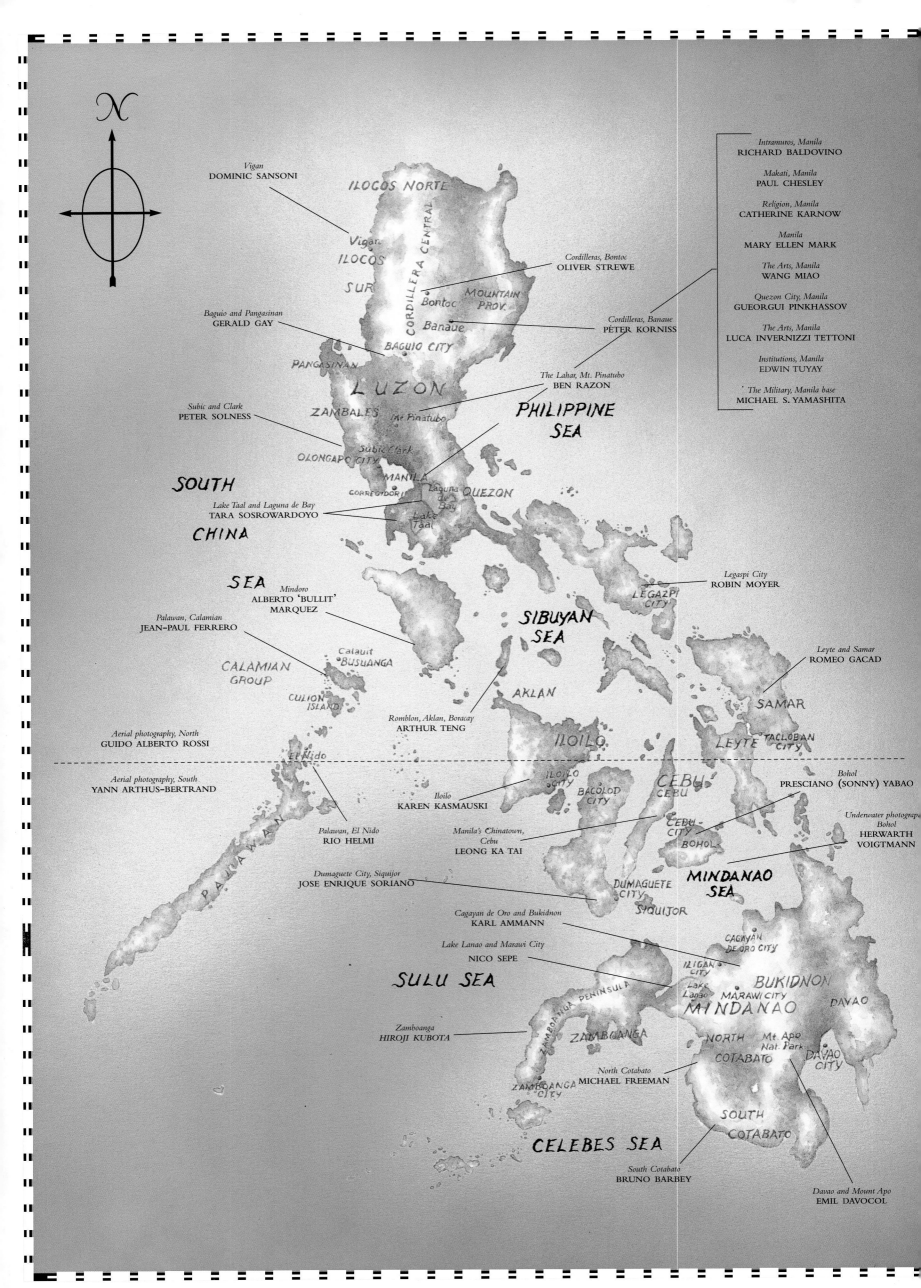

N

Vigan
DOMINIC SANSONI

ILOCOS NORTE

Intramuros, Manila
RICHARD BALDOVINO

Makati, Manila
PAUL CHESLEY

Religion, Manila
CATHERINE KARNOW

Manila
MARY ELLEN MARK

The Arts, Manila
WANG MIAO

Quezon City, Manila
GUEORGUI PINKHASSOV

The Arts, Manila
LUCA INVERNIZZI TETTONI

Institutions, Manila
EDWIN TUYAY

The Military, Manila base
MICHAEL S. YAMASHITA

Vigan
ILOCOS
SUR

CORDILLERA CENTRAL

Cordilleras, Bontoc
OLIVER STREWE

MOUNTAIN
PROV.

Bontoc

Banaue

Cordilleras, Banaue
PÉTER KORNISS

Baguio and Pangasinan
GERALD GAY

BAGUIO CITY

PANGASINAN

LUZON

PHILIPPINE
SEA

The Lahar, Mt. Pinatubo
BEN RAZON

Subic and Clark
PETER SOLNESS

ZAMBALES

Mt. Pinatubo

Subic Clark

OLONGAPO CITY

MANILA

CORREGIDOR

QUEZON

Laguna
de
Bay

SOUTH

Lake Taal and Laguna de Bay
TARA SOSROWARDOYO

Lake
Taal

CHINA

SEA

Mindoro
ALBERTO 'BULLIT'
MARQUEZ

Legaspi City
ROBIN MOYER

LEGAZPI
CITY

SIBUYAN
SEA

Palawan, Calamian
JEAN-PAUL FERRERO

Calauit
BUSUANGA

CALAMIAN
GROUP

CULION
ISLAND

AKLAN

Leyte and Samar
ROMEO GACAD

SAMAR

Aerial photography, North
GUIDO ALBERTO ROSSI

Romblon, Aklan, Boracay
ARTHUR TENG

ILOILO

LEYTE

TACLOBAN
CITY

El Nido

Aerial photography, South
YANN ARTHUS-BERTRAND

ILOILO
CITY

Iloilo
KAREN KASMAUSKI

BACOLOD
CITY

CEBU
CEBU

Bohol
PRESCIANO (SONNY) YABAO

Underwater photograp
Bohol
HERWARTH
VOIGTMANN

Palawan, El Nido
RIO HELMI

PALAWAN

Manila's Chinatown,
Cebu
LEONG KA TAI

CEBU
CITY

BOHOL

Dumaguete City, Siquijor
JOSE ENRIQUE SORIANO

DUMAGUETE
CITY

MINDANAO
SEA

Cagayan de Oro and Bukidnon
KARL AMMANN

SIQUIJOR

Lake Lanao and Marawi City
NICO SEPE

CAGAYAN
DE ORO CITY

SULU SEA

ZAMBOANGA PENINSULA

ILIGAN
CITY

Lake
Lanao

BUKIDNON

MARAWI CITY

MINDANAO

DAVAO

Zamboanga
HIROJI KUBOTA

ZAMBOANGA

NORTH
COTABATO

Mt. Apo
Nat. Park

DAVAO
CITY

North Cotabato
MICHAEL FREEMAN

ZAMBOANGA
CITY

SOUTH
COTABATO

CELEBES SEA

South Cotabato
BRUNO BARBEY

Davao and Mount Apo
EMIL DAVOCOL

DIARY OF THE JOURNEY

Two hundred million years ago the islands of the Philippines were spewed up from the bottom of the ocean by the hot violence of volcanoes. These pieces of land now lie scattered like a vast jigsaw across the waters of the South China, Philippine, Sibuyan, Celebes and Sulu seas. Each land mass holds a clue to the diverse and colorful picture that is this archipelago nation. The question in the minds of Marina Mahathir, Project Director, and Didier Millet, Publisher, in January of 1994 was *how do we capture such a picture?*

This was a question Marina had first asked herself following two business trips to Manila, each one year apart—the scale of change within the city in just 12 months was so impressive that Marina felt the scene should be captured for all the world to see. Good pictures, of all types, require money and so getting some pesos together was the first task on Marina's list, but first she had to enlist interest and support—that was where Doris Magsaysay Ho, Chief Executive Officer of Manila-based Magsaysay Lines, came in. In March 1994 Editions Didier Millet and Against All Odds Productions were busy putting together *Passage to Vietnam* out of their Bangkok headquarters. Editions Didier Millet flew Doris over to watch the coordinators, logistics staff and photographers in action. Doris was suitably impressed by the organized chaos and immediately brought in Manila-based PR consultant Henrietta Bolinao (known as Bon-jin) to draw up a list of possible sponsors for the million-dollar project, tentatively entitled *Seven Days in the Philippines*. Bon-jin and Doris then suggested names for an Editorial Advisory Board to direct the financing and editorial and pictorial content of the book. President Fidel V. Ramos was approached and asked to support the project which he did without reservation.

Marina, Bon-jin and Peter Schoppert, Editions Didier Millet's Editorial Director, then embarked on an 18-month odyssey through the offices of the most powerful and successful companies in the Philippines. Over 70 boardrooms later they had gathered together more than 30 enthusiastic sponsors to give the project money and support. The financial go-ahead was given to Didier in Singapore and he called an Editorial Advisory Board meeting and appointed Alfredo Roces, editor of *Filipino Heritage*, the most comprehensive series of books on Filipino culture ever produced, as the Editorial Consultant.

Peter and Alfredo sat down in the lobby of the Westin Philippine Plaza two weeks later with a huge map of the Philippines spread over several tables—much to the amusement of the waitresses and other guests. They then began the huge task of attempting to divide this country into 35 pieces—a piece for each photographer. After a week Peter and Alfredo were satisfied that they had made "a good start" by dividing the country up geographically and they departed for Singapore and Australia respectively with a daunting idea of the massive organizational task

KAREN KASMAUSKI   MICHAEL S. YAMASHITA

that lay ahead of them. Peter returned a month later with Jill Laidlaw, Project Editor, to meet Raul Teehankee, newly-appointed by Alfredo to direct logistics on the 35 assignments. Ten Assignment Coordinators were duly enrolled from photographic, tourism, and editorial backgrounds to research and structure the initial assignments supplied by Peter and Alfredo. In the following two months the assignment coordinators reported to Raul as they organized trips to nature reserves, visits to tribal peoples, tours of monuments and factories, expeditions up mountains and dives beneath the ocean. The coordinators were in turn backed up by the staff of the Philippine Convention and Visitors Corporation guided by Raul. Raul then reported to Jill and Peter in Singapore and the assignments' progress was carefully monitored on paper, via phone and fax.

By September 1995 Didier and Marina had invited the 35 photographers, the main logistical preparations had been made, the 35 assignments had been researched, and Marina, Peter, Irene Tan, Travel Coordinator, and Jill were on their way to Manila with computers, files, and three weeks of last minute arrangements before them. A suite in the Westin Philippine Plaza was quickly turned into a Nerve Center—soon re-named the Nervous Center as the shoot week drew ever closer—and, by October 4th, the Raw Nerve Center. American photographer Paul Chesley, and Indonesians Rio Helmi and Tara Sosrowardoyo were the first lensmen to arrive. The trickle of photographic talent soon became a flood and by Glenda Baretto's welcome

cocktail party at the Via Mare restaurant on the evening of October 6th guests at the Westin were becoming used to seeing photographers laden with tripods, lenses and cameras staggering through the lobby.

On October 7th the photographers and project staff donned the traditional Barong Tagalog shirt and headed off in a motorcade for a lunch thrown by President Ramos in their honor at the Malacañang Palace. After a buffet of traditional Filipino food President Ramos gave the *Seven Days* team a personal tour of the palace and encouraged the photographers to tee off with him into the Pasig River. By the time the *Seven Days* team left Malacañang in the late afternoon there was hardly time to change for a celebration dinner, entitled Barrio Fiesta, held at the Philippine International Convention Center organized by the Department of Tourism and the Philippine Convention and Visitors Corporation. Photographers and staff were greeted by songs and music and dinner was followed by an evening of musical theatre and traditional dancing in a supreme display of Filipino hospitality.

The party was fantastic—but many photographers were cursing it at around 5am the following morning as they shook off their couple of hours of sleep and headed out of Manila and on to their assignments. For the photographers, the work had just begun. The project team got up late, had the first leisurely breakfast they had had in a month and then drifted into the Raw Nerve Center to man the phones and wait for the first problems to arise "on the road". As the week progressed the photographers began to report back—a delighted

TARA SOSROWARDOYO

PETER SOLNESS

GUEORGUI PINKHASSOV

RIO HELMI

*T*op: President Ramos catches up on paperwork; Marina Mahathir and the First Lady pose with some of the female members of the team. Bottom: Peter Schoppert, Jill Laidlaw and Paul Sision at work in the Nerve Center; Didier Millet heads off to Corregidor; Alfredo Roces meets President Ramos; Didier, Mary Ellen Mark and Carmen Guerrero Nakpil at Glenda Baretto's welcome cocktail party; Raul Teehankee and Bon-jin Bolinao on their way to the lunch; Luca Tettoni shoots inside the Palace.

RAUL TEEHANKEE

MICHAEL S. YAMASHITA

PETER SOLNESS

GUEORGUI PINKHASSOV

TARA SOSROWARDOYO

KARL AMMANN

TARA SOSROWARDOYO

BRUNO BARBEY

CATHERINE KARNOW

GUIDO ALBERTO ROSSI

BRUNO BARBEY

Mike Yamashita raved about the 1,000 Philippine Army cadets who turned out on parade just for him; Péter Korniss declared his intention to move to the village of Bugnay after he was serenaded by a chorus of young girls on the final night of his assignment; and Edwin Tuyay reported his wife giving birth on October 11th, at 1.30am—we christened his daughter the Shoot Week baby, Edwin called her Nirvana.

As the end of the shoot week approached Janie Bennett (newly arrived from Tokyo) began to prepare for the debriefing sessions. Tired photographers, drivers and guides began making their way back to the Westin on Saturday 14th and Marina, Peter, Janie and Jill began checking in film, taking notes on predictions for 'the really great shot,' and getting roll notes together. By lunchtime the next day everyone was ready for a bit of rest and relaxation and the team headed off *en masse* to the Sun Cruises ferry terminal in Manila Bay for a two-day trip to Corregidor Island. After tanning by the pool, sightseeing, and dinner and dancing our seven days in the Philippines was brought to an end with the very thing that started it all off—good old fashioned Filipino hospitality.

Top: Catherine Karnow edges out Bruno Barbey to get the President on film; Karen Kasmauski tees off at the Malacañang Golf Club; Paul Sison, coordinator, calls back to the Nerve Center while out on assignment; Justin Nyuda, coordinator, calls back to Manila from Mindanao; President Ramos takes a swing; Didier, Marina and the President collect golf balls; Bon-jin, Marina, Jill and Marina's daughter, Ineza, on their way to Corregidor; Shirley Low (right) and Irene Tan on a tour of Corregidor Island; President Ramos takes a shot. Below: The editorial and photographic team outside the Malacañang Palace.

PETER SCHOPPERT

245

THE PHOTOGRAPHERS

Karl Ammann, Switzerland/Kenya
A former hotelier who developed a passion for photography, Ammann is now resident in Nanyuki, Kenya, where he concentrates his efforts on capturing African wildlife on film. His publications include *Cheetah* (1984), *The Hunter and the Hunted* (1988) and *Masai Mara* (1990). Karl's photographs have won world recognition, including three World in our Hands awards from the BBC Wildlife Photographer of the Year competition. Karl is actively involved in ape conservation, has just completed a book on the three gorilla sub-species, and is known internationally as an expert on Africa's bush meat trade.

Yann Arthus-Bertrand, France
Paris-based photographer Yann Arthus-Bertrand is one of the world's most prolific aerial photographers. Arthus-Bertrand's work has been published in more than 40 books and in magazines such as *Geo*, *National Geographic*, *Paris Match* and *Life*. Yann's all-absorbing project of the moment is, *Earth From Above: An aerial portrait on the eve of the year 2000*, a Unesco-backed enterprise that aims to provide a comprehensive picture library of the world from above. Yann, as the principle photographer on the project, has the daunting task of flying over as many countries as possible before the end of the century to photograph the state of our planet. Yann's pictures will be used for environmental studies, educational purposes and special publications.

Richard Baldovino, Philippines
Richard Baldovino started his photographic career as a photojournalist with the Philippine News Service in 1957 and then became a freelance journalist on daily newspapers and weekend magazines. In 1963 Richard began his travels all over Southeast Asia, Europe, the Middle East, the United States and Australia as a photographer for *Asia Magazine*. He then branched out into advertising, art books and corporate publications. In 1993 Richard was recognized by the city of Manila for his contribution to arts publications in the Philippines. Richard is currently working on publications about the artists Felix Resurreccion, Francisco Hidalgo, Arturo Luz, Jose Joya and Ed Castrillo.

Bruno Barbey, France
Bruno Barbey was born in Morocco in 1941. He has covered stories on every continent and has photographed the conflicts in Biafra, Vietnam, Israel, Kurdistan, Ireland and Kuwait. Barbey's work is regularly published in books and as major photo essays in international magazines such as *Time*, *Life*, *Stern*, *National Geographic*, *Paris Match* and *GEO*. He has received numerous awards for his photographic achievements, including the Overseas Press Club Award and the Missouri Photojournalism Award. Bruno's work has been exhibited in Europe, USA and Japan and can be found in national and private collections from Paris to New York.

Paul Chesley, USA
Paul Chesley has been a freelance photographer with *National Geographic* since 1975 and has completed over 35 projects worldwide with the Society. Solo exhibitions of his work have appeared in museums in London, Tokyo, New York, Washington, DC and Honolulu. His photographic essays are also regularly featured in *Life*, *Fortune*, *GEO*, *Stern*, *Newsweek* and *Time*. Chesley has participated in 14 *Day in the Life* book projects, as well as other recent publications such as *Thailand: Seven Days in the Kingdom*; *Indonesia: A Voyage Through the Archipelago*; *Malaysia, Heart of Southeast Asia*; *Mauritius*; *Passage to Vietnam*; and *Bangkok*.

Emil Davocol, Philippines
Emil spent ten years working in publications, design and photography before setting up his own company in 1987. His Light Images Photography and Design produces calendars, posters, annual reports and advertising visuals. Davocol won awards for excellence in advertising photography and Camera Club photography in 1992 and 1995 and has been regularly involved in photo exhibitions and large-scale photographic books since 1977. Emil has recently set up a digital imaging studio, Pixel Inc. He was a participant in the photographic book *Brunei: Abode of Peace* and photojournalist for the PATA-Gold awardee *Times Travel Library: Manila* in 1991.

Jean-Paul Ferrero, France/Australia
French-born Jean-Paul started taking photographs of animals and wildlife in 1973. His work has now been featured in *National Geographic*, *GEO*, *International Wildlife*, *American Natural History*, and *Australian Natural History*. Jean-Paul migrated to Australia in 1982 and founded the Auscape International picture library. Jean-Paul now travels in Australia, Southeast Asia, Africa and the Antarctic regions for six months of every year. Apart from taking pictures of wild animals, he tries to spend more time taking landscape photographs with a large format camera. The remainder of the year is taken up with writing captions and selling his work to magazines, publishers and advertising agencies.

Michael Freeman, Britain
After six years in advertising, Michael made a break for photography in 1971 and traveled up the Amazon. The resulting pictures were used by Time-Life books. Freeman became a full-time photographer in 1973 and moved on to become the principal photographer for the *Smithsonian* magazine. He published his work internationally, making a specialty of Southeast Asia. In 1990 Houghton Mifflin published his book on Cambodia, *Angkor: The Hidden Glories*, the first account on these temples in more than 20 years. He has written 23 books on photography and his recent *Photography Workshop* series was awarded the Prix Louis Philippe Clerc by the French Ministry of Culture. In 1995 Freeman wrote, directed and launched *Virtual Photography*, the first fully interactive multimedia CD-ROM on photography.

Romeo Gacad, Philippines
Romeo Gacad began his photographic career as a staff photographer for his high school paper in 1975 and then moved on to work for the New York- and Paris-based picture agency, Sygma. In 1985 Romeo set up the Agence France-Presse photo service in Manila to cover domestic and international news events. The new agency cut its teeth on the People Power revolution which led to the downfall of President Ferdinand Marcos in 1986, as well as the turbulent six years of Corazon Aquino's rule that followed. Romeo has covered Filipino coup attempts, earthquakes and volcanic eruptions and has still managed to photograph stories in the Middle East, Cambodia, Vietnam, Indonesia, Brunei, Japan, Singapore, Australia and New Zealand.

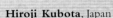
ROMEO GACAD

Gerald Gay, Singapore/Australia
After graduating with a Diploma in Fine Arts (Photography) from Prahran College of Advanced Education in Melbourne, Australia, in 1982, Gerald worked as a freelance photographer before setting up Through the Lens Productions in 1992. His company's work includes advertising and industrial photography as well as corporate and editorial assignments for clients such as American Express, Citibank, Royal Brunei Airlines, Civil Aviation Authority of Singapore and Richard Ellis. Gerald's work has been exhibited in Australia and Singapore and his photographs have been published all over the world.

Rio Helmi, Indonesia
Bali-based Rio Helmi began working as a photographer in 1978, shooting mainly in black and white film and focusing on the lifestyles of indigenous people of Indonesia. After running a virtual one-man-show at the *Sunday Bali Post*, Rio worked as photographer and associate editor for the Indonesian media group, Sinar Kasih. In 1983 he went freelance and since then his work has appeared in magazines all over the world. He has also worked on film productions, press promotions, and advertising. Rio has several large format photographic books to his name, including *River of Gems* and *Bali Style*. In 1989 he was Chief Photographer on the book *Indonesia: A Voyage Through the Archipelago* and he currently runs Image Network Indonesia.

Catherine Karnow, USA
Born and raised in Hong Kong, the daughter of an American journalist, Catherine Karnow has been traveling all her life. She developed a serious interest in photography in high school and began spending her summers in Europe photographing and working at Magnum Photos in Paris and London's *Sunday Times Magazine*. She graduated from Brown University in 1983 with degrees in literature and filmmaking. After a brief stint as a film-maker Karnow turned to stills photography full time. Her work appears regularly in *GEO*, *Smithsonian*, *Islands* and *Figaro*. Her book projects include: *Passage to Vietnam*, the *Day in the Life* series, the Insight Guides to Washington, DC, Provence, France and Los Angeles, and *Adventures on the Scotch Whisky Trail*.

Karen Kasmauski, USA
Karen Kasmauski is a contract photographer with *National Geographic* and has produced 11 major stories for the magazine since 1984. Karen particularly enjoys working in Southeast Asia and her stories in the region include: an examination of the sociology of Japanese women; coverage of Japan's economic role in Asia; a special feature on Ho Chi Minh City; and coverage of the Kobe earthquake. Kasmauski photographed the book *Hampton Roads* and has contributed to several book/CD-ROM projects, including *Passage to Vietnam* and *Women in the Material World*. Her work on Japanese women is being developed into a CD-ROM. She is married with two children, Will, who is five and Katie, who is three.

Péter Korniss, Hungary
Péter was born in Kolozsvár, Transylvania in 1937 but moved to Budapest, Hungary in 1949 to study law. Péter's academic career was cut short during the 1956 Revolution, when he was expelled from university. Péter took up photography in 1958 when working on a weekly picture magazine. He later became Picture Editor of the magazine. Péter has been freelancing since 1991. At the beginning of his photographic career Péter worked with ballet and folklore groups, before turning to the disappearing traditional peasant life and culture of eastern Europe. He has been concentrating on this subject for 28 years, mostly in his homeland of Transylvania.

Hiroji Kubota, Japan
Hiroji Kubota was born in Tokyo in 1939 and earned a BA in Political Science from Waseda University in 1962. After graduating Hiroji left Japan to live in the United States for six years. On his return to Tokyo in 1967 Hiroji's first major project documented Okinawa before its return to Japan. In 1975 Hiroji's coverage of the fall of Saigon led him to concentrate on Asia. 1978 was spent photographing North Korea, a project that he only completed in 1987. From 1979-85 Hiroji photographed China, and 1988 was spent photographing Myanmar (Burma). From 1989-1992 Kubota's lens was turned on *all* of the United States. Hiroji's current project, *Out of the East*, is a study of all the countries that lie between Myanmar and Korea.

Leong Ka Tai, Hong Kong/Singapore
Ka Tai gave up his first career as an engineer to work in a photographic studio in Paris for three years. On his return to Hong Kong in 1976, Ka Tai set up his own studio, Camera 22. Since 1982 he has concentrated on travel, editorial and corporate photography projects. Ka Tai has exhibited in numerous group exhibitions and in eight one-man shows. His pictures have been published in over 20 books and in magazines such as *GEO*, *Stern*, *Time*, *Newsweek*, *National Geographic*, *Forbes*, *New York Times Magazine* and London's *Sunday Times Magazine*. Ka Tai was voted artist of the year in 1991 by the Hong Kong Artist Guild and was awarded the first prize for Best Photojournalism in 1995 by the Harry Chapin Media Awards, New York.

Mary Ellen Mark, USA
Mary Ellen Mark has achieved worldwide visibility through her numerous photo-essays and portraits in magazines such as *Vogue*, *Harpers Bazaar*, *Life*, *Fortune*, *Allure*, *Rolling Stone*, *US Magazine*, *Stern*, *New York Times Magazine* and *The Sunday Times Magazine* (London). For over two-and-a-half decades, she has dedicated herself to taking pictures that reflect a high degree of humanism. In 1994 she was awarded the John Simon Guggenheim Fellowship, the Matrix Award for outstanding woman in the field of film/photography, and the Dr. Erich Salomon Award for outstanding merits in the field of journalistic photography. She has published 11 books and has photographed several advertising campaigns — among which are British Levis, Coca-Cola, Coach Bags, Keds, Hasselblad, Heineken and Mass Mutual.

Alberto 'Bullit' Marquez, Philippines
Bullit became a photographer when he joined the staff of the University of the Philippines college publication. He later freelanced for leading magazines and newspapers before joining the Associated Press in Manila as Chief Photographer. Bullit has covered stories all over the region, including the Seoul Olympics, the Pope's visit to Indonesia, Australia and Manila in 1990, the turmoil in China, and the elections in Cambodia. Bullit was awarded a citation by the Associated Press Managing Editors for his coverage of the cyclone in Bangladesh in 1990 and was awarded Travel Photo of the Year by the Kalakbay Awards Foundation. Bullit's work has been published in 11 books and he has exhibited his work in New York, Manila and Tokyo.

GUEORGUI PINKHASSOV

STEPHEN PAGE

Robin Moyer, USA

Robin Moyer is *Time* magazine's Chief Photographer in Asia. During his 25-year career he has won many prestigious awards, including the World Press Photograph of the Year (1982) and the Overseas Press Club Robert Capa Gold Medal Citation for Courage and Enterprise for his work covering the war in Lebanon. Robin has made special portraits of most of the major political and business leaders in Asia and has led teams of photographers in the coverage of major stories for *Time*, including the People Power revolution in the Philippines, the Seoul Olympics and the Japanese emperor's funeral. In addition to his work in photojournalism, his personal work has been purchased by the Library of Congress for its Masters of Photography Collection.

Gueorgui Pinkhassov, Russia/France

Moscow-born Gueorgui first became interested in photography at the end of his secondary schooling. From 1969-1971 he trained as a cameraman at the Soviet Cinema Institute and then worked at Mossfilm studios. 1978 was an eventful year: Gueorgui became an independent artist after joining Moscow's Graphic Arts Union. Between 1978 and 1985 he did reportage for various Soviet publishing houses and worked as the stills photographer on Andrei Tarkovski's film *Stalker*. Gueorgui has taken part in numerous exhibitions since his move to Paris in 1985. He joined Magnum in 1988 and won a grant from the French Ministry of Culture for his work on minority groups in the USSR. Gueorgui works in various formats, including color, black and white, and Polaroid.

Ben Razon, Philippines

After two years of study at the Art Institute of Pittsburgh, USA, Ben started out as a freelance photo assistant in New York City in 1981. On his return to the Philippines 18 months later he did reportage for the *Philippine Daily Globe*, covering the Mount Pinatubo eruption and the American military pullout from the Subic and Clark bases. Ben is currently working as a contributing photographer for various publications such as *Entertainment Now* and *Financial Executive Digest*, and as a freelance commercial photographer for Fuji Film, Metro Pacific Land and One Asia Capital Investment. Ben's personal photographic projects concentrate on human interest stories; he has spent time documenting the plight of lahar victims and Amerasian children in the Zambales and Pampanga provinces of the Philippines.

Guido Alberto Rossi, Italy

At the start of his career in 1967, Guido Rossi concentrated on photojournalism—the Middle East, the Vietnam War, and Indochina. In 1973 he returned to his native Milan and concentrated on travel and sports photography. His hobby—flying small planes—soon developed into an obsession; Guido now combines work and play and is recognized as one of the world's foremost aerial photographers. Since 1978 he has been director of Image Bank, Italy, and his work appears regularly in magazines all over the world and in books such as *Over Singapore*, *Over Indonesia*, *Over Malaysia*, and *Indonesia: A Voyage Through the Archipelago*.

Dominic Sansoni, Sri Lanka

After studying art in England, Dominic Sansoni returned to his native Sri Lanka and became involved in news and war photography. He has worked for a variety of international news and feature magazines. Sansoni's warm and sensitive pictures of Asian peoples have appeared in *Time* and *Asiaweek*. He is one of the stalwart photojournalists always invited to contribute to creative photography books, such as *Malaysia, Heart of Southeast Asia*, *Indonesia: A Voyage Through the Archipelago*, and *Sri Lanka: The Resplendent Isle*. Dominic lives in Colombo and runs an art gallery and picture library.

Dominico Garcia Sepe, Philippines

Dominico was born in Mindanao, Philippines. He grew up in Manila and began to take photographs during his high school years. He went to college in Baguio City, took up mechanical engineering, and became a photographer and artist for the college paper. In 1985, only one year shy of getting his degree, 'Nico' packed up his camera and left for Marag Valley, Cagayan, a war-torn area then called 'No Man's Land'. Here, Nico began eight years of freelance photography, covering the nation's refugee camps, squatter colonies, and disaster-stricken villages. He has worked on various book and calendar projects, a one-man show and collective exhibitions, and continues to take pictures for local publications and non-governmental organizations.

Peter Solness, Australia

Peter Solness is one of Australia's most respected photojournalists. He began his career as a part-time surfing photographer back in the mid-1970's at the age of 16. After completing photographic studies in the early 1980s he took to the road with a motorcycle and a camera, and spent two years documenting Australia and its people. Peter's formative training as a photojournalist was during the mid-1980's while working as a photographer for the *Fairfax Press*, the *Sydney Morning Herald*, and the *National Times*. Since going freelance in 1988, Peter's work and interests have taken him to many locations, including China, South America, the Pacific, Southeast Asia, Eastern Europe, the USA, Russia and the former USSR.

Jose Enrique Soriano, Philippines/Singapore

Born in Manila, Derek first learned photography from his father, who, in his teens, was a labman for one of Manila's oldest publishing houses. In 1985, at the age of 19, he became a news photographer documenting social conditions in the country and worked for the *Philippine Daily Express*, *The Observer*, *Philippine Daily Globe* and *Newsday*. After seven years of working for newspapers, Derek shifted to magazines, shooting portraits and travelogues for *Philippine Panorama* and *Metro Magazine*. At the same time, he started his personal documentary projects, among them the plight of Amerasian children. For the past three years Jose has photographed life in a mental institution. He moved to Singapore in 1994 and established Alaya Photos, a picture agency which specializes in photojournalism and commercial work for the Asian region.

JEAN-PAUL FERRERO

Tara Sosrowardoyo, Indonesia
Tara was born into a diplomat's family in New York City and was raised all over the world. In 1976, he made a name for himself as an album cover art director and photographer. Tara has always found it impossible to specialize: he has done (or still is doing) advertising, aerial, corporate, editorial, journalistic, fashion and portrait photography. His greatest love is photographing people. He has exhibited extensively, and his work has appeared in *The New York Times, Time, Newsweek, Businessweek, Asiaweek, Vogue* and *Marie Claire*. His books include *Indonesia: A Voyage Through the Archipelago; Pusaka: Art of Indonesia;* and *Passage to Vietnam*. Tara is represented by Gamma Liaison/Liaison International in New York and Q-Photo in Tokyo. He lives mostly in Jakarta, Indonesia.

Oliver Strewe, New Zealand/Australia
Oliver Strewe began taking photos in the early 1970's and took part in his first group exhibition in 1972 in London. Other exhibitions have featured Australian workers and tattoo artists as subjects. Most recently he curated and contributed to *East Timor: 1942 to 1992*. Oliver has photographed extensively in the Pacific, documenting most of the recent independence movements from PNG to the uprising in Vanuatu. He has been the principal photographer on 11 book projects, covering such diverse subjects as wines of California to the beach culture of Bondi, Sydney. Oliver's photojournalism has featured in cover stories for both Australian and foreign newspapers and magazines such as *GEO, The New York Times Magazine* and *Merian*.

Arthur Teng, Malaysia
Arthur took his first picture in 1968 with a borrowed camera and owned his first 'serious' camera in 1981. Now he spends all the time he can spare (from his full-time job as a graphic artist) traveling in search of perfect pictures. He has won awards in competitions such as the Nikon Photo Contest International, the Canon Asia Photo Contest, Asia Magazine's Photo Contest, Photo Asia Rally, Ballantine's Finest International Photography Award and ACCU World Photo Contest. Between 1988 and 1990 Arthur was appointed Nikon's official photographer in Malaysia. Arthur's work has featured in numerous publications; in four solo exhibitions in Malaysia and one in Denmark; and in *Eyes on Asean*, a traveling photo exhibition (1992).

Luca Invernizzi Tettoni, Italy/Singapore
Luca left Italy in the mid-seventies to travel in India and Indonesia and eventually settled in Thailand where he worked for 15 years as an advertising, corporate and editorial photographer. Luca's main interest has always been Asian art and archaeology, and his impressive photographic record of Thai archaeology has led to the publication of several books, such as the *Arts of Thailand, Arts of Southeast Asia,* and *The Prasat Museum*. He is better known, however, for his house and garden books: *The Tropical Garden, Balinese Gardens, Thai Style, Thai Style Gardens, Sarawak Style,* and a number of books on Asian cookery. Luca now lives in Singapore where he runs his photo-library, Photobank.

Edwin Tuyay, Philippines
Edwin Tuyay started off his photographic career as a stills photographer for local and international film productions. In 1986 he joined the *Manila Chronicle* as a staff photographer. In 1988 Edwin was sent to the Spratly Islands by *Asiaweek* to do an Eyewitness Pictorial. After this assignment Edwin was hired by *Asiaweek*—as their first staff photographer. Based in Manila, Edwin shoots covers, editorials, corporate and eyewitness pictorials for the magazine. He freelances for *Esquire, Forbes, Time, Asia Magazine* and *Filipinas Magazine*. His book credits include *Mount Pinatubo: 500 Years After, Eyes on Asean* and *Philippines: Spirit of Place*. Edwin is represented in Japan by Pan Asia Newspaper Alliance and in New York by Gamma Liaison.

Herwarth Voigtmann, Germany/Maldives
Herwarth Voigtmann—as much a professional diver as a professional photographer—likes to spend as much time as possible in deep water. He left his native Germany to start a scuba-diving school on the Salerne Gulf in 1971. Since then, Herwarth has photographed beneath every ocean on the planet and his spectacular pictures of sharks have won him international acclaim. He runs his own dive resort on Maaya Fushi island in the Maldives.

Wang Miao, China/Hong Kong
Wang was one of the founders of April Photo Meet, and the Modern Photo Salon, two of the first private professional photographers' organizations in China. She has worked as a photographer for the Weinwu (Historical Relics) Press and as a reporter for the China News Service and Hong Kong China Tourism Press. Wang's first successful exhibition, *Tibet Through My Eyes*, was held in Hong Kong in 1986; followed in 1987 by *A Journey Through Sichuan and Tibet* in California. In 1988 Wang had her first one-woman show, *The China Photographers Series Exhibition: The Individual Works of Wang Miao* in Taiwan. At present Wang is the Vice Director of Hong Kong China Tourism Press and Editor-in-Chief of *China Tourism*.

Presciano (Sonny) Yabao, Philippines
Sonny Yabao specializes in arts and travel photography for Manila's glossy magazines. Yabao's photographs have appeared in regional publications such as *Asia Magazine, Asiaweek, Orientations* and *Metro*. He has been a photo editor for the daily Philippine paper *Newsday,* for the Department of Tourism, and for *Lifestyle Asia* magazine. In 1990 he was named Photojournalist of the Year by the National Press Club, San Miguel Corporation and the Press Photographers of the Philippines. Sonny received the Most Outstanding Achievement Award from the organizers of National Photography Week and was a medalist at the 51st International Salon in Japan. Sonny's work has been published in Southeast Asia, most recently in photographic books such as *Eyes on Asean, Philippines: Spirit of Place,* and *Tagaytay: Town on the Ridge*.

Michael S. Yamashita, USA
Michael began taking pictures in 1971 while on a 'roots' trip to Japan. What started as a hobby led to a career that has taken him to six continents and combined his two passions—photography and travel. He has lived and worked in Singapore, Thailand, Hong Kong and Japan. He shoots for a variety of Japanese publications and has been a regular contributor to *National Geographic* since 1979. His publications include *In the Japanese Garden* and *The Mekong: Mother of Waters*. He has participated in four *Day in the Life of* book projects and has received a variety of awards from the National Press Photographers Association Pictures of the Year competition; the New York Art Directors Club and the Asian-American Journalists Association.

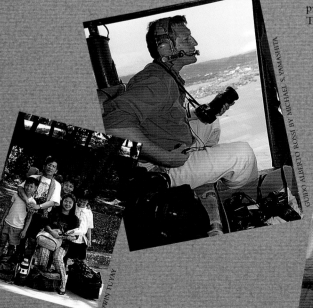

GUIDO ALBERTO ROSSI BY MICHAEL S. YAMASHITA

EDWIN TUYAY

CATHERINE KARNOW

249

STEPHEN PAGE

THE AUTHORS

CATHERINE KARNOW

ALFREDO ROCES, *Editorial Consultant*
Alfredo is a freelance writer, painter, photographer and journalist who has been based in Sydney, Australia, since 1978. His biography on the Philippine National Artist Cesar Legaspi won the Manila Critics Circle Book of the Year award in 1993. Alfredo was Editor of Australian *GEO* from 1978 to 1991. Prior to his move to Australia Alfredo was Editor-in-Chief of a ten volume study of Filipino culture and history, *Filipino Heritage* (1978). Alfredo spent ten years as a daily columnist for the Philippines' leading newspaper, *The Manila Times*, and was named Columnist of the Year by the Citizens Council for Mass Media in 1971.

JONATHAN BEST, *Early Images*
Jonathan Best works in Manila as curator of photography, rare books, and maps for the Geronimo Berenguer de los Reyes, Jr. Foundation. Jonathan has a B.A. in Art History from New College at Hofstra University. He has curated several exhibits of Philippine photography including the opening exhibit at Malacañang Heritage Museum in 1993. In 1994 he authored the book, *Philippine Picture Postcards: 1900-1920*, and is presently set to publish a sequel covering American colonial photography in the Philippnes.

ALEJANDRO R. ROCES, *Fiesta Islands*
A former Secretary of Education of the Republic of the Philippines, Dr. Alejandro Roces has a distinguished reputation as a scholar of Filipino fiestas and is also well known for his journalism and short stories. Alejandro contributes to magazines such as *Arizona Quarterly*, *Southwest Review*, *Pacific Spectator* and the *New Mexico Quarterly* in the United States and *Hemisphere* in Australia. New anthologies of his short stories and textbooks are about to be published in the United States and Australia.

JAMES HAMILTON-PATERSON,
History Tells The Story
James Hamilton-Paterson was educated at Oxford, where he won the Newdigate Prize for poetry. In addition to extensive journalism for the *Sunday Times*, *The Times Literary Supplement*, he has published books of fiction, non-fiction and poetry. He has written extensively about the sea in *Playing With Water* and *Seven-Tenths*. His novel, *Gerontius*, won him the Whitbread First Novel Award in 1989. Most recently he has published a novel about the Philippines, *Ghosts of Manila*, and a collection of stories, *The Music*.

RODRIGO D. PEREZ III, *Chapter Introductions*
Rodrigo D. Perez, III (Dom Bernardo Maria, OSB) is a monk of the Benedictine Abbey of Manila and Rector of San Beda College. He earned a B.S in architecture in 1953 and worked as a freelance writer. Rodrigo then worked as a set and lighting designer and stage manager in the theatre. He worked for the government tourist office for six years and in 1962, at the age of 30, he became a Benedictine monk, and was ordained a priest in 1969. He has recently written numersous articles on Philippine architecture.

ELIZABETH V. REYES, *Captions*
Elizabeth V. Reyes' career as an arts and features writer has taken her to the United States to graduate in journalism from Syracuse University (New York) and to participate in Stanford's Professional Publishing course. Elizabeth has traveled all over the Philippines as a roving author and editor and spent ten years in Singapore as editor of the magazines *Singapore Tatler*, *Business Traveller*, and *Signature Magazine*. Elizabeth's recent work as an author has included travel guides to Bali and Manila. Elizabeth was publishing manager of *Tagaytay: Town on the Ridge*, and is project coordinator of Archipelago Press' forthcoming title, *Filipino Style*.

JEAN-PAUL FERRERO

SELECT BIBLIOGRAPHY

Cesar Adib Majul, *Muslims in the Philippines*, University of the Philippines Press, Quezon City 1973

Teodoro A. Agoncillo and Milagros C. Guerrero, *History of the Filipino People*, R.P. Garcia Publishing Co., Quezon City, fourth edition 1973

Teresita Ang See, *The Chinese in the Philippines: Problems and Perspectives*, Kaisa Para Sa Kaunlaran Inc., Manila 1990

Jose S. Arcilla, *Recent Philippine History 1898-1960*, S.J. Ateneo de Manila University 1991

Manuel Blanco, *Flora de Filipinas*, 2 vols., second edition 1845, reprinted by Eugenio Lopez Foundation, Rizal 1993

Raymond Boner, *Waltzing with a Dictator*, Times Books, New York 1987

Theodore Friend, *Between Two Empires, the Ordeal of the Philippines 1929-1946*, Yale University Press 1965

Juan Gatbonton, editor, *Art Philippines*, The Crucible Workshop, Manila 1992

Nick Joaquin, *A Question of Heroes*, Ayala Museum, Manila 1977

Nick Joaquin, *Prose and Poems*, Graphic House, Manila 1952

Stanley Karnow, *In Our Image: America's Empire in the Philippines*, Random House, New York 1989

Jose Rizal, *Noli Me Tangere*, English translation by Charles E. Derbyshire, Philippine Education Co. 1958

Alejandro R. Roces, *Fiesta*, Vera-Reyes Inc., Manila 1980

Alfredo Roces, editor, *Filipino Heritage: The Making of a Nation*, 10 vols., Lahing Pilipino Publishing Inc., Manila 1978

Alfredo and Grace Roces, *Culture Shock Philippines*, Times Books International, Singapore, second edition 1985

F. Sionil José, *The Pretenders*, Solidaridad Publishing House, Manila 1962

Marilies Von Brevern, *Faces of Manila: Thirty Authentic Filipino Lifestories*, Manila 1985

Leon Wolff, *Little Brown Brother*, Doubleday & Co., Inc., New York 1961

PHOTOGRAPHY INDEX

aerial photography
Yann Arthus-Bertrand   63, 66-7, 68, 80, 255, 256
Rio Helmi   title, 239
Guido Alberto Rossi   imprint, 46-7, 49, 62, 69, 80, 145, 164
Tara Sosrowardoyo   144
Oliver Strewe   63
Aquino, Corazon
Catherine Karnow   126-7
actors
Villaroel, Carmina
Dominic Sansoni   102
Revilla, Bong
Tara Sosrowardoyo   232
artists
Bencab
Gerald Gay   232
Cajipe-Endaya
Luca Invernizzi Tettoni   232
Luz, Arturo
Catherine Karnow   232
Olmedo, Onib
Wang Miao   232
Ayala, Don Jaime Zobel de
Paul Chesley   153

Badjao people
Bruno Barbey   43
baptism
Edwin Tuyay   98-9
beauty contests
Paul Chesley   225
Catherine Karnow   220, 222
Karen Kasmauski   220, 224

Catholics and churches
Romeo Gacad   104-5
Rio Helmi   92-3, 116
Leong Ka Tai   86-7, 94, 95
Mary Ellen Mark   124, 125
Robin Moyer   102-3
Gueorgui Pinkhassov   38
Dominic Sansoni   93
Presciano (Sonny) Yabao   100
Central Bank Mint
Edwin Tuyay   150
Central Plain
Guido Alberto Rossi   69
children
Yann Arthus-Bertrand   59
Richard Baldovino   211
Paul Chesley   half title, 42, 45, 201, 211
Romeo Gacad   211
Catherine Karnow   203, 211
Karen Kasmauski   186-7
Mary Ellen Mark   124, 125
Alberto 'Bullit' Marquez   211
Robin Moyer   200
Gueorgui Pinkhassov   200, 206, 211
Dominic Sansoni   210, 211
Peter Solness   150, 208-9
Arthur Teng   211
Edwin Tuyay   188-9, 204-5
Herwarth Voigtmann   211
clubs and dancing
Paul Chesley   240
Romeo Gacad   226
Luca Invernizzi Tettoni   240
Catherine Karnow   226, 227, 228-9
Mary Ellen Mark   185
cockfighting
Bruno Barbey   84-5
Paul Chesley   241
Hiroji Kubota   216
Cojuangco, Imelda
Mary Ellen Mark   185
construction
Romeo Gacad   162-3
Gueorgui Pinkhassov   163
Corregidor Island

Guido Alberto Rossi   39
Peter Solness   156
crafts
Tara Sosrowardoyo   108-9
directors
Castillo, Celso Ad
Gerald Gay   233
Padilla, Nonon
Luca Invernizzi Tettoni   232

El Shaddai
Rio Helmi   113
Catherine Karnow   112-13
elderly people
Edwin Tuyay   180, 181, 218-19

faith healing
Catherine Karnow   120-21, 122-23, 239
Mary Ellen Mark   124
fashion
Paul Chesley   221
Ramos, Barge
Luca Invernizzi Tettoni   233
Sotto, Inno
Catherine Karnow   223
Moreno, Pitoy
Mary Ellen Mark   232
fiestas
Paul Chesley   236
Emil Davocol   237
Romeo Gacad   236
Karen Kasmauski   212
Hiroji Kubota   212, 213
Mary Ellen Mark   234
Robin Moyer   213
Edwin Tuyay   236
Presciano (Sonny) Yabao   236, 237
firefighting
Leong Ka Tai   140-41
fishing
Karl Ammann   54-5
Bruno Barbey   52
Alberto 'Bullit' Marquez   137
Jose Enrique Soriano   60
Tara Sosrowardoyo   61, 178
Presciano (Sonny) Yabao   53
funerals
Paul Chesley   99
Mary Ellen Mark   124

golf
Yann Arthus-Bertrand   63
Oliver Strewe   63

hairdressing
Leong Ka Tai   182-3
Mary Ellen Mark   184
Ho, Doris Magsaysay
Leong Ka Tai   161
horses
Paul Chesley   196-7
Michael Freeman   216
hospitals
Edwin Tuyay   180
hotels
Paul Chesley   254
Emil Davocol   254
Tara Sosrowardoyo   148, 254
Ifugao people
Oliver Strewe   121
Iglesia ni Cristo
Catherine Karnow   111
industry
Presciano (Sonny) Yabao   165
jeepneys
Paul Chesley   145
Rio Helmi   cover, 240
Luca Invernizzi Tettoni   146-7
Dominic Sansoni   166-7
Jesus is Lord Church
Rio Helmi   115

Kalinga people
Péter Korniss   81
lahar
Catherine Karnow   71
Ben Razon   70-71
Peter Solness   71
lechon
Richard Baldovino   174, 240
Paul Chesley   175
Leyte
Romeo Gacad   contents, 89
Luzon
Guido Alberto Rossi   49, 69, 164
Michael S. Yamashita   12-13

Macapagal, Diosdado
Catherine Karnow   128
Mangyan people
Alberto 'Bullit' Marquez   168-9, 171, 179, 217
Manila
Catherine Karnow   143, 154
Gueorgui Pinkhassov   44, 88, 144
Guido Alberto Rossi   149
Manobo people
Emil Davocol   36, 241
Marcos, Imelda
Catherine Karnow   129
markets
Michael Freeman   176
Leong Ka Tai   177, 190-91
Gueorgui Pinkhassov   176
Jose Enrique Soriano   173
Michael S. Yamashita   177
Mindanao
Karl Ammann   54-5
Yann Arthus-Bertrand   59, 80
Bruno Barbey   10-11, 50-51, 52, 56-7
Nico Sepe   58
music
Nono, Grace
Luca Invernizzi Tettoni   232
Ayala, Joey
Wang Miao   233
Robin Moyer   200
Dominic Sansoni   240
Muslims
Hiroji Kubota   117, 118-19
Nico Sepe   58, 117

nuns
Catherine Karnow   126-7
Dominic Sansoni   214-15

Palawan
Jean-Paul Ferrero   64, 65
Rio Helmi   endpapers
Guido Alberto Rossi   46-7, 62
Pasig River
Gueorgui Pinkhassov   134-5
Philippine Airlines
Paul Chesley   157, 158-9, 254
Philippine military
Guido Alberto Rossi   130
Michael S. Yamashita   130-31
plantations
Bruno Barbey   74
Emil Davocol   77
Michael Freeman   76
Karen Kasmauski   75

Ramos, Fidel V., President
Bruno Barbey   245
Karen Kasmauski   244
Peter Solness   244
Tara Sosrowardoyo   245
Michael S. Yamashita   138-9
rice
Romeo Gacad   78-9, 172
Péter Korniss   80
Guido Alberto Rossi   80
Oliver Strewe   239
Presciano (Sonny) Yabao   136

Rizal, Jose
Catherine Karnow   240
Edwin Tuyay   37
Samar
Romeo Gacad   104-5, 170
San Agustin Museum
Richard Baldovino   107
Santa Niños
Luca Invernizzi Tettoni   241
Dominic Sansoni   114
schools
Paul Chesley   192
Gueorgui Pinkhassov   88
Dominic Sansoni   34
Edwin Tuyay   132-3
sculptors
Pilapil, Impy
Luca Invernizzi Tettoni   232
Lluch, Julie
Wang Miao   231
Orlina, Ramon
Wang Miao   233
Saprid, Solomon
Gueorgui Pinkhassov   106
shipping
Leong Ka Tai   161
Gueorgui Pinkhassov   160
Sin, Cardinal
Catherine Karnow   90-91
sport
Romeo Gacad   193
Mary Ellen Mark   202
Gueorgui Pinkhassov   194-5
Jose Enrique Soriano   198
Edwin Tuyay   199
Stock Exchange
Catherine Karnow   151, 152
Subic Bay
Peter Solness   155

T'boli people
Bruno Barbey   10-11, 50-51, 56-7

traffic and transport
Leong Ka Tai   143
Catherine Karnow   142
Alberto 'Bullit' Marquez   41

underwater photography
Herwarth Voigtmann   60-61

Vigan
Dominic Sansoni   110
Tara Sosrowardoyo   101
Visayas
Arthur Teng   48
Presciano (Sonny) Yabao   68
volcanoes
Robin Moyer   8-9, 72-3, 241
Guido Alberto Rossi   68

weddings
Rio Helmi   96-7
Wang Miao   239
wildlife
Karl Ammann   83
Emil Davocol   241
Jean-Paul Ferrero   82-3
Rio Helmi   endpapers, 82
Arthur Teng   82
Presciano (Sonny) Yabao   83
writers
Moreno, Virginia
Mary Ellen Mark   232
Alcantara, Odette
Wang Miao   233
Caruncho, Eric
Wang Miao   230
Sionil José, "Frankie"
Wang Miao   233

Zamboanga
Yann Arthus-Bertrand   40, 59, 66-7
Bruno Barbey   84-5

THE SPONSORS

Gold

Philippine Airlines (PAL) takes pride in having one of the most extensive networks in the region, and an international route system that reaches the US mainland, Western Europe, the Middle East, Southeast and Northeast Asia, and Australia. Philippine Airlines is gearing up for the expansion and modernization of its fleet beginning with the new Boeing 747-400 and Airbus 340 aircraft which will have 'skybeds', fully reclining First Class seats, skyphones, and individual TV monitors in First Class and Business Class. Other types of aircraft arriving which feature state-of-the-art technology are the Airbus 330 and the Airbus 320.

The **Philippine Tourism Authority** (PTA) is a corporate entity attached to the Department of Tourism (DOT) and it is committed to developing both the international and domestic tourism industry in the Philippines. The PTA develops tourist zones and operates and maintains tourist facilities throughout the Philippines. These facilities include a dive resort, beach resorts, golf clubs, a national park, hot springs and youth hostels. In addition to these activities the PTA provides assistance to tourism investors and project proponents and generates additional revenue to fund national and corporate tourism development requirements.

Fil-Estate Land, Inc. traces its business roots back to 1981 when it was formed to market the projects of other real estate establishments. Since then, the company has ventured into developing its own projects, carving a name for itself as a creator of world-class, innovative and trendsetting communities. Today, the acknowledged leader in the Philippine real estate industry, Fil-Estate stands as an active partner in nation-building and as a citizen committed to the preservation of the world's ecological balance.

PILTEL (Pilipino Telephone Corporation), since its inception in 1968, has become the Philippines' leader in wireless telecommunications. Now a publicly-listed, full service telecommunications firm, PILTEL is a major player in three telecommunications market segments. Its Mobiline service has installed a new and powerful Motorola network which will soon be aided with the latest in cellular digital technology known as Code Division Multiple Access or C.D.M.A.; its Beeper 150 service has captured the electronic paging market with its alphanumeric, numeric and audionumeric services; and its Fixed Telephone Service covering eight (8) local exchanges outside Metro Manila and its newly designated service area in southern Mindanao.

Kodak Philippines is a subsidiary of the Eastman Kodak Company. It has been in operation since 1928 and is today the undisputed leader in the local photographic industry. Substantially a marketing company, Kodak Philippines carries imaging products that meet a wide variety of customer needs, not just in the realm of picture-taking and film processing but also in recording, storing, transmitting and delivering image outputs. Our products range from futuristic photo discs to visual presentations, high resolution x-ray films, digital analyzers for the clinical diagnostics industry, sophisticated microfilm equipment and high capacity, state-of-the-art copiers.

The Westin Philippine Plaza, Manila's premier business resort hotel, is set in the 12-acre parkland within the Cultural Center of the Philippines Complex. All 612 guestrooms, including 47 suites, have balconies allowing panoramic views of Manila Bay's world-famous sunset; each room is equipped with color television, IDD phones, airconditioning, and an electronic security system. The 13 function rooms include the Grand Plaza Ballroom covering 14,976 square feet of unpillared floorspace. Facilities include four restaurants, six bars, a two-storey entertainment center, state-of-the-art Health Club, four championship tennis courts, ten-hole driving range by the bay, and a spectacular lagoon-shaped swimming pool.

Universal Motors Corporation (UMC) pioneered in the assembly and distribution of automobiles starting with Mercedes Benzes. A two-decade partnership with Nissan was forged in the '70s with the assembly and distribution of Datsun (former name of Nissan) passenger cars. In the early '80s, Nissan divided its product line between UMC and Pilipinas Nissan Inc. (now Nissan Motor Philippines, Inc.), with UMC concentrating on the production of Nissan light commercial vehicles. Today UMC continues to enjoy much vigor and dynamism by consistently providing the market with quality products in the Nissan *Patrol Safari*, *Eagle* pickups and the Nissan *Terrano*.

After the People Power revolution, the Aquino government gave the Department of Tourism the authority to establish and operate a tax and duty free merchandising system in the Philippines. As a division of the Philippine Tourism Authority, **Duty Free Philippines** contributes over 60% of the entire government budget for tourism infrastructure. To date, DFP operates 14 outlets all over the country. It offers more than 50,000 world-class products, making it one of the most successful duty free operators in the Asia Pacific region. DFP has won numerous international awards and recognition and at the end of 1995 was ranked the world's fourth largest duty free shop.

Silver

A. Soriano Corporation (ANSCOR) was founded by Don Andres Soriano in 1930 as a family corporation engaged in real estate, securities investment, insurance, and general merchandizing. The company today is a widely diversified conglomerate with ventures in mining, steel, paper, fertilizers, telecommunications, container port services, construction and engineering, power generation, banking and financial services, cargo handling, cement wires and cables, and travel and tourism. The company manages four charitable foundations which aid victims of disease and natural disasters and help organize rural cooperatives and educational and medical programs.

Ayala Corporation, a highly diversified conglomerate, was established in 1834 and is one of the oldest and most respected commercial groups in the Philippines. Ayala is also one of the largest listed companies on the Philippine Stock Exchange. The Corporation has been long acknowledged as the Philippines' foremost real estate developer. Synonymous with Ayala's name is Makati City in Metro Manila, which it developed to become the Philippines' premier financial district and a showcase of successful integrated urban planning and development. Ayala's business portfolio includes interests in real estate, financial services, food and agribusiness, insurance, telecommunications, electronics and information technology, and international operations.

Coca-Cola Bottlers Philippines, Inc. (CCBPI) is the world's first joint-venture Coca-Cola bottler, established in 1981 by The Coca-Cola Company and San Miguel Corporation (which had been bottling Coca-Cola since 1927.) CCBPI is one of the ten largest Coca-Cola bottlers in the world, and by far the country's leading soft beverage company with 75% of the Philippine market. In the global Coca-Cola network, CCBPI has gained a reputation for excellence and innovation, particularly in the fields of sales and marketing, product quality, human resource development, and environmental management.

Established in 1947, the **Development Bank of the Philippines** (DBP) is the country's premier development bank with an authorized capital of US$ 191 million and assets of over US$ 2.57 billion. The bank is not only a major source of medium and long-term funds for power, telecommunications, transportation, agriculture, education and health care, but is also the country's major conduit of international funds from multilateral and bilateral institutions, programs and grants. DBP provides a wide range of wholesale and retail banking services through its branch network, as well as accredited participating financial institutions which serve as its conduits for countryside development.

Equitable Banking Corporation (EBC) was established on September 26th, 1950. A few months after it was conceived, it became the first commercial bank to be licensed by the one-year-old Central Bank of the Philippines. In 1988, EBC was granted a universal banking license by the Central Bank. A year after, EBC became one of the four charter members of an ATM consortium now known as the Megalink Group. Moreover, EBC has organized its capabilities along corporate, consumer, merchant and international banking lines to meet the more specialized requirements of specific segments of both business and consumer sectors. Likewise, EBC has established wholly-owned subsidiaries for credit cards, foreign exchange, technology, insurance brokerage and investment activities. At present, it has a branch network of 45 Metro Manila branches, 28 provincial branches and one foreign branch in Hong Kong.

The ***International Herald Tribune*** (IHT) was founded in Paris in 1887 as the European edition of the *New York Herald*. From its founding, it gained rapid influence in the international community and has become the newspaper of record for people of stature and education throughout the globe. Today the IHT is owned by the *New York Times* and the *Washington Post*, the premier daily publications in the United States. The IHT remains headquartered and centrally edited in Paris and is now printed simultaneously in 12 world centers, namely Hong Kong, Singapore, Tokyo, Bologna, Frankfurt, London, Marseilles, Paris, the Hague, Toulouse, Zurich and New York. With a daily readership of 500,000 in over 181 countries, the IHT is the first truly global newspaper.

The **JAKA Group** is a conglomerate engaged in investment management, real estate property management and development, production of safety matches, forestry plantation management, product distribution, food production and marketing, security services, air and land transportation, social development and overseas investment. Headed by Jack Enrile as President and Chief Executive Officer, JAKA is composed of 38 companies with assets of PhP 5.2 billion and 3,800 employees, with JAKA Investments Corporation as the Group's flagship. From its beginnings as a small family company in 1974, JAKA has become one of the fastest-growing and more profitable conglomerates in the Philippines, known for its extensive real estate properties and the wide variety of products it distributes or manufactures.

One of the Philippines' top five corporations, **Meralco** distributes electricity to a quarter of the Philippine population based in the National Capital Region, industrial estates, and the suburban and urban areas of adjacent provinces. The biggest of 146 electric distribution utilities in the Philippines, it is a publicly owned corporation with the second biggest number of stockholders in the country. Through strategic alliances and partnerships, it has diversified into power generation, power plant rehabilitation, business process reengineering and information technology consultancy, and real estate development. Incorporated in 1903, it is one of 200 emerging market firms worldwide.

The **National Steel Corporation** (NSC), formerly a government-owned corporation, is one of the Philippines' biggest corporations with assets of over 35 billion pesos. The prime producer of flat and long products in the country, NSC has four major operating facilities in Mindanao and Luzon, namely: the Billet Steelmaking Plant, producing billets; the Hot Mill, producing hot rolled coils and plates; the Cold Mill, producing cold rolled coils and tin mill black plates; and Electrolytic Tinning Lines, producing tinplates. NSC was recently privatized with the Malaysian-based Wing Tiek Holdings Berhad and their Filipino partners as majority investors.

Pearl Farm Beach Resort is the premier resort destination in the Philippines today. It has been the recipient of the Resort of the Year award for two consecutive years in the annual Department of Tourism Kalakbay Awards—known as the 'Oscar' of the country's tourism industry. Pearl Farm, a tropical paradise that teems with deluxe amenities, is located in Davao Province in the becoming islands of Mindanao. The resort has become a favorite destination in the region among tourists from both Asia and Europe.

Petron Corporation is the market leader in the Philippine oil refining and marketing industry. It has the distinction of having maintained uninterrupted market leadership in the industry for two decades now. A nationwide distribution network provides Petron with the ability to deliver various types of petroleum products to its storage terminals, industrial clients, service stations and LPG dealers all over the country. Petron's shareholders include Philippine National Oil Company, the most diversified energy company in the Philippines; Saudi Aramco, the world's largest producer and exporter of crude oil; and thousands of individual and corporate investors. Today, Petron has the biggest shareholder base from any Philippine IPO.

The **Philippine Amusement and Gaming Corporation** (PAGCOR) is the government agency that operates and manages casinos in the Philippines. PAGCOR runs Casino Filipino branches in Manila, Pasay, Laoag, Angeles, Olongapo, Tagaytay, Cebu, Bacolod, and Davao. Games offered are blackjack, baccarat, pai-gow, roulette, big & small, craps, stud poker and slot machines. The hospitable and friendly atmosphere at Casino Filipino has made it a favorite gaming destination of international highrollers. PAGCOR's earnings are used to fund development programs ranging from education to sports, as well as to assist civic and charitable projects.

Created by law to hold and conduct charity sweepstakes, races, lotteries and other similar activities, the **Philippine Charity Sweepstakes Office** is the principal government agency in the Philippines engaged in health and welfare-related programs and investments. These projects and activities are aimed at providing permanent and continuing sources of funds for health programs, medical assistance and services, and charitable grants.

The ***Philippine Daily Inquirer*** was founded in 1985. It is the daily newspaper with the biggest audited circulation in the Philippines today, with sales reaching nearly a quarter of a million copies. Based in Metro Manila, the *Inquirer's* 137 staff and its 90 correspondents in three news bureaus in Luzon, the Visayas and Mindanao cover and report the news from all parts of the country. With its balanced reporting and fearless commentary, the *Inquirer* has won 70 journalism awards in the past ten years. It has landed in the list of the top 1,000 corporations in the Philippines every year since 1987.

Founded on November 28th, 1928, the **Philippine Long Distance Company** (PLDT) is the Philippines' principal provider of domestic and international telecommunications services. Its charter (which extends to 2028) authorizes it to provide virtually every type of telecommunications service including basic telephone and toll services, digital leased lines, and a host of other value-added services. PLDT operates the country's only worldwide microwave long distance network. It provides international long distance services using two international gateways, submarine cables, and satellite systems that connect PLDT's nationwide network to 227 international destinations.

Shell's partnership with the Filipino people dates back to 1914. Business then largely involved the importation and sale of kerosene needed by household consumers in Manila and outlying areas. Through the decades, Shell's business operations have expanded from manufacturing and distribution of refined petroleum products to chemicals and liquefied petroleum gas production. In recent years, Shell has also ventured into oil and gas exploration in line with the country's objective of achieving self-sufficiency in its energy requirements. Recognizing the increasing demand for petroleum products, Shell has constructed a bigger and more modern refinery, which began operations in February 1995.

Puerto Azul Land, Inc. (PALI) is a real estate, leisure and tourist estate development company. With a substantial land area of 338 hectares, PALI is moving to realize its vision of building a world-class satellite city with a mix of residential, resort, leisure, commercial and marina facilities. PALI's initial projects are Vista De Loro Heights, a community of luxury condominium units with one of the most scenic views in Puerto Azul; Las Quintas Residences, residential lots specially designed with individual cluster driveways and green buffer zones; Altamira Subdivision, lots located on the fingers of a high mountain ridge; and The Wharf, a development which features a yacht club, ferry terminal and residential condominium units.

As one of the Philippines' most highly integrated retailing groups, the **Rustan's** group of companies includes a premier chain of upscale department stores, supermarkets, gourmet shops, restaurants, duty-free commercial centers, speciality stores, and a nationwide distribution network for quality merchandise. In the Philippines, the name Rustan's is synonymous with retailing. In its nearly five decades of operations Rustan's, primarily through its department stores, and additionally through its formidable network of companies, has helped to define the fledgling science of retailing in the Philippines and in the Southeast Asian region, through a standard of operational and merchandising excellence that is second to none.

San Miguel Corporation is the largest food, beverage and packaging company in the Philippines. Founded in 1890 as a small brewery, the company and its subsidiaries today generate 4% of the country's gross national product and is the nation's biggest private employer with over 30,000 employees. The company's principal businesses are beverages, food and agribusiness, and packaging. San Miguel beer holds 81% of the domestic market and is among the world's largest selling beer brands. San Miguel's manufacturing operations extend to Hong Kong, China, Indonesia, Vietnam and Taiwan, and its products are exported to over 30 countries around the world.

The **Yuchengco Group of Companies** (YGC) is one of the largest business conglomerates in the Philippines. The Group provides integrated financial services and has diversified operations in banking, general and life insurance, investment banking, finance and leasing, property development, pre-need services and investments in agricultural and commercial activities. The Group's major flagships are Rizal Commercial Banking Corporation, House of Investments Inc., Malayan Insurance Co., Inc., and Great Pacific Life Assurance Corporation.

ABS-CBN is the pioneering broadcast leader in the Philippines. According to annual surveys conducted by the *Asian Business Magazine* since 1991, the network is the "Most Admired Media Company" in Asia. The *Far Eastern Economic Review*, in its own surveys, lists ABS-CBN in the Top Five Companies in the Philippines and one of the leading 200 companies in Asia. Through the years, the network has been a consistent winner of major international awards in creative excellence. ABS-CBN's satellite news, entertainment and educational broadcasts reach two-thirds of the world, all in service to the Filipino.

The **Department of Tourism** (DOT) is the primary government agency tasked to encourage, promote and develop tourism as a major socio-economic activity with the support of both the private and public sectors. In addition, it undertakes to ensure the safe, convenient and enjoyable stay and travel of the country's domestic and foreign tourists. DOT's functions are geared towards making the tourism industry an important contributor to the country's national growth. Basically, it formulates programs and projects that develop and promote the Philippine tourism industry here and abroad. The DOT aims to entice more tourists to the country to help increase the country's earnings and generate employment opportunities.

Distributed Processing Systems Incorporated (DPSI), known as the exclusive distributor of Apple computers and peripherals in the Philippines, is definately more than just a computer sales and service firm. By continuously anticipating information technology market needs, DPSI creates solutions to suit the specific needs of clients, and supports them through its diverse divisions. Now in its 14th year, DPSI has also ventured into a number of non-media industries such as dentistry, security systems, food flavoring, and others.

Since its establishment in 1948, **Magsaysay Lines, Inc.** (MLI) has been committed to the development of the shipping industry in the Philippines. It is involved in shipowning, ship operation, manning, crewing and agencies. Its vessels service domestic, regional and worldwide distribution of cargo. Magsaysay takes pride in its tradition of providing services that conform to the highest-standards of excellence and customer satisfaction.

Ogilvy & Mather is the fastest growing multinational agency in the Philippines. And is rapidly being recognized as one of the most creative—placing second in the most recent Creative Guild rankings. The company is one of the leading international advertising agencies with 272 offices in 62 countries, and is part of the largest marketing services group in the world.

The **Philippine Convention & Visitors Corporation** (PCVC) is the marketing arm of the Department of Tourism. Its main task is to promote the Philippines as a tourist, convention and incentive travel destination. The PCVC is a non-stock, non-profit government corporation and is open to entities, groups and individuals with any interest in tourism. PCVC offers marketing services consisting of sales and promotions activities, promotional material support, bid assistance and liaison services for congresses and special events. PCVC is a member of selected international organizations based in key markets abroad. These affiliations place PCVC in the mainstream of developments in the international travel and convention industry.

Shangri-La's Mactan Island Resort is situated on a tropical landscaped site in Mactan Island, Cebu, Philippines. With direct flights to and from major cities in Asia the Resort is 15 minutes from the airport. The Resort features 359 rooms, a private beach, 1,500 square meter multi-level pool and a variety of watersports. For corporate events and parties a ballroom and function rooms are available. Four restaurants and three bars offer Asian and Continental buffets and fine dining.

LOGISTICS AND SUPPORT

A project the size of *Journey Through the Archipelago* takes the resources and manpower of a big budget film to complete. None of the photographers could have made it through their assignments without the help and support of a cast of thousands—literally.

The photographers start the shoot week as they mean to go on.

RIO HELMI

A Coordinator calls back to the Westin Nerve Center from his UMC car via PILTEL (left).

TARA SOSROWARDOYO

PAUL CHESLEY

PAL pilots ferry our photographers to the Philippines from all over the world (center). Kodak keeps us well supplied with film (left). Pearl Farm in Davao was a popular stopover for many Mindanao-based photographers (below).

GUEORGUI PINKHASSOV

Magsaysay Lines' Sun Cruises transport the Project Team to Corregidor Island (below left). Puerto Azul was a favorite destination (below).

GUIDO ALBERTO ROSSI

YANN ARTHUS-BERTRAND

EMIL DAVOCOL

PAUL CHESLEY

TARA SOSROWARDOYO

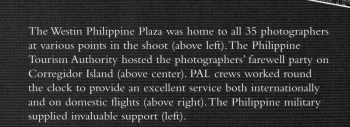

The Westin Philippine Plaza was home to all 35 photographers at various points in the shoot (above left). The Philippine Tourism Authority hosted the photographers' farewell party on Corregidor Island (above center). PAL crews worked round the clock to provide an excellent service both internationally and on domestic flights (above right). The Philippine military supplied invaluable support (left).

PETER SOLNESS

ACKNOWLEDGEMENTS

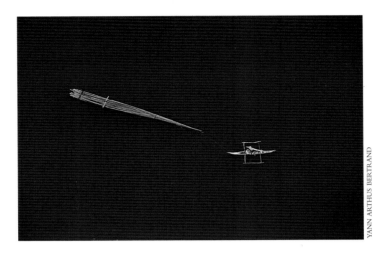

YANN ARTHUS BERTRAND

at Nissan Universal Motors Corporation

Glenn C. Balane, Overall Coordinator ◆ Marcel Chiu, Communications and Spare Parts Support ◆ Joey Arenas, Provincial Assignment Coordinator ◆ Minda Torres, Dispatch and Vehicle Control ◆ Luis Beza ◆ Ruben Clemente ◆ Bernard Cureg ◆ Joselito Galuz ◆ Leo Lopez ◆ Antonio Maglaque ◆ Salvador Nicmic ◆ Lorenzo Portugal ◆ Eldred Prelejera ◆ Danilo Susano ◆ Bernard Untalan ◆ Vicente Valderueda ◆ Noel Raymundo ◆ Fernando Reyes ◆ Roman Reyes ◆ Ramon Villanueva ◆ Demetrio Villondo ◆ Carlos Lorica ◆ Jonathan M. Aguilar, Deployment Planning Coordinator ◆ Cris Bayani, Logistics Support ◆ Ador Bugarin, Service Support ◆ Linda B. Castillo, Vehicle Requirement ◆ Dan Andrew Cura, Vehicle Requirement and SWAT Assistance ◆ Mara Gabot, Logistics Support ◆ Rodrigo T. Janeo, Jr., Vehicle Requirement ◆ Romeo Mallari, Official Photo Coverage ◆ Alex Martinez, Depot of Units

at Piltel Mobiline

Ramon O. Cojuangco, Jr., President and Chief Executive Officer ◆ Edmigio V. Ramos, Marketing Director ◆ Ditas Lopez

at the Philippine Convention & Visitors Corporation

Daniel G. Corpuz, Overall Coordinator ◆ Bernadette I. Lazaro, Deputy Executive Director Corporate Affairs ◆ Stanie D. Soriano, Manager, Corporate Relations Department ◆ Ferdie Capistrano, Finance ◆ Naomi D. Cruz, Secretariat ◆ Jeannie M. Sundario, Secretariat ◆ Liway Baretto, Secretariat ◆ Joji Gregorio, Air Transport ◆ Jay Guinto, Security ◆ Rafael Relucio, Security ◆ Leah Castillo, Security ◆ Jun de Los Reyes, Airport Reception and Cargo Facilitation ◆ Ewitt Pagdanganan, Administrative Services ◆ Liz Agulla, Social Functions ◆ Venus Tan, Social Functions

Location Guides

Annie F. Balboa ◆ Rey Bascon ◆ Janet Canoy ◆ Resty Dimacuha ◆ Ellen Fajardo ◆ Linda Fernandez ◆ Ligaya Gomez ◆ Teresita R. de Luna ◆ Grace Mandani ◆ Teresita Mauricio ◆ Nuani Mulingbayan ◆ Susan Del Mundo ◆ Marietta S. Santillan ◆ Ana P. Seneres ◆ Cesar Topacio ◆ Jojo de Veyra

Support Staff

Lorna Adlawan ◆ Jojo Alcantara ◆ Bert Alcazura ◆ Boyet Cabansag ◆ Mandy Cabansag ◆ Angge Calalang ◆ Jet Calalang ◆ Cenon Crecencio ◆ Bong Ducusin ◆ Oscar Elep ◆ Celly Faustino ◆ Arnold Gonzales ◆ Thelma Molina ◆ Josie Molo ◆ Moonyeen Mutia ◆ Caloy Orogo ◆ Nanding Ramoran ◆ Isaiah Salva ◆ Marivic Toledo ◆ Boy Vilan ◆ Von Zarsadias

at the Office of the President, Malacañang Palace

Undersecretary J. Apolinario L. Lozada Jr., Appointments Secretary and Assistant for Foreign Affairs ◆ Major Catalino S. Cuy, Executive Assistant ◆ Consol Eduardo M. R. Menez, Director IIII ◆ Atty. Doy Lucenario, Presidential Protocol Office ◆ G. Anjo A. Siose, Technical Assistant, Appointments Office ◆ Gary Guntang, Technical Assistant, Appointments Office ◆ Isabella Marissa C. Favis, Administrative Officer, Appointments Office

at the Philippine Armed Forces

Secretary Renato de Villa, Secretary of National Defense ◆ Lourdes I. Ilustre, Officer in Charge, Office for Public Affairs ◆ Lt. General Arnulfo Acedera, Commanding General, Philippine Air Force ◆ Brig. Gen. Eduardo T. Cabanlig, President, National Defense College of the Philippines ◆ Major Dominador Aquino and all the pilots of 205 Airwing ◆ Col. Percival M. Subara, Commander, 3rd Marine Brigade ◆ Brig. Gen. Ponciano Millena, Commander Marine Forces, Southern Philippines ◆ Marlyn Manicsic, Secretary to the President, National Defense College of the Philippines

at Philippine Airlines

Lucio C. Tan, Chairman and Chief Executive Officer ◆ Manolo E. Aquino, Executive Vice President, Administration and Services ◆ Mila Abad, Vice President, Advertising and Marketing Support ◆ Annie de Leon

at Kodak Philippines

Michelle Andrea T. Arville, Imaging Consultant, Professional and Printing Imaging ◆ Nestor Martin C. Marfori, Jr., Country Business Manager, Professional, Printing and Publishing Imaging ◆ Jose F. Diño, Jr, Country Business Unit Manager, Professional and Printing Imaging

at The Westin Philippine Plaza

Michel Geday, former General Manager ◆ John F. Swaney, General Manager ◆ Sandra D. Garcia, Director of Sales and Marketing ◆ Zenaida M. P. Iglesias, Director of Public Relations and Advertising ◆ Ria Nakpil, Reservations Manager

on Photographic Assignments

Dr. Rainerio Abad, Delgado Memorial Hospital ◆ Richard J. Gordon, Governor of Subic Bay Metropolitan Authority ◆ Edo and Annabelle Adriano ◆ Edgar Allan Agaton, Nissan Branch Manager, Dumaguete ◆ Nonnette C. Bennett, Cordillera News Agency ◆ Ben Cabrera, artist ◆ Dr. Milagros Cantre, Delgado Memorial Hospital ◆ Constancio Fe A. Casaba, Jr., Subic Bay Metropolitan Authority ◆ Lori Crespo, Logistics Support and guide, El Nido ◆ Danny Dolor ◆ Sohura Dimaamtro ◆ Arnulfo Efren D. Dizon, Clark Development Corporation ◆ Jun L. Encarnacion, hairdresser ◆ Captain Elmer Estilles, guide ◆ Dean Erlinda S. Fernandez, CCP Outreach, Kalibo, Aklan ◆ Edgardo M. Geraldo, guide ◆ Tommy D. Hafalla ◆ Lina Jose ◆ Cristina Lapres, Provincial Tourism Office, Bacolod City ◆ Leni Mascardo, Provincial Tourism Office, Dumaguete ◆ Jong Mendoza, photographer's assistant ◆ Pitoy Moreno, fashion designer ◆ Don Morgan and The Firehouse Club ◆ Grace Ozoa, Marine Biologist, Siliman University Marine Laboratory ◆ Estela Pagsuyuin, *Asiaweek* ◆ Glenn G. Peralta, Department of Tourism, Legaspi City ◆ Ma. Victoria Rufino ◆ Ricky Reyes, hairdresser ◆ Mars Rubinos, guide ◆ Rene Sanchez ◆ Marissa Segovia, guide ◆ Mrs Julie Rufino and The Sparklers Club ◆ Hans-Juergen Springer ◆ Claude Tayag, artist ◆ Nonong Tumada ◆ Ellen Tuyay and Nirvana ◆ Rea Yamsuan, El Nido guide ◆ Datu Udang and family of the Bagobo tribe ◆ Mia Pelayo ◆ Frank Villaraiz, Department of Tourism, Davao ◆ Keith Garcia ◆ Virginia Baco ◆ Annie Ringor ◆ Rufus Bellamy ◆ Abigail Jacob ◆ Cora Jacob ◆ Philippine Veterans Association ◆ Amateur Boxing Association of the Philippines ◆ Bienvenida ◆ Sabrina ◆ Bianca ◆ Suleiman ◆ Norma Morrante ◆ Isagani Granale ◆ Promis Lagrimas ◆ Roberto Delgado ◆ Reynaldo Sambiri ◆ Paul Kasimpan

with Special Thanks to

Eduardo P. Pilapil, Secretary of Tourism ◆ Rizalino Navarro, Secretary of Trade and Industry ◆ Vicente Carlos, Secretary of Tourism (1993-95) ◆ Rep. Manuel A. Roxas ◆ Pangasinan Governor Oscar Orbos ◆ Doris Magsaysay Ho ◆ Rolando Mario and Monique Villonco ◆ Antonio and Linda Lagdameo ◆ Carlos Dominguez ◆ Peter D. Garrucho ◆ Antonio and Armita Rufino ◆ Carmencita Tantoco-Lopez ◆ Ma-an B. Hontiveros ◆ Rodolfo Cuenca, Sr. ◆ Freddie S. Alquiros ◆ Isabelita Sy ◆ The Philippine Print and Broadcast Media ◆ Alan Ortiz ◆ Antonio O. Cojuangco

On the way to market with a precious cargo of wood—the building blocks of the villages of Zamboanga.

Three farmers dwarfed by the landscape cut down their crops to form a patch-work of color when seen from the air.